Praise for *A Real Apprentice*

"Jesus used stories, pictures, an[d] hitting truths. Discover these un[...] and they could transform your [...]

BOBBY BALL, BRITISH COMEDIAN,

"The reality of our love for Jesus is measured not by the intensity of our songs and prayers, but by the way we live Monday through Sunday. Graham Warner, a former colleague of mine, has always been radical in his approach to discipleship. Here, he explores what it means to live by Christ's commands today. A must read for all serious followers of Jesus."

GRAHAM KENDRICK, CHRISTIAN SONGWRITER; COMPOSER OF "KNOWING YOU," "AMAZING LOVE," "SHINE JESUS SHINE," AND MANY OTHER POPULAR WORSHIP SONGS

A Real Apprentice

a real apprentice
101 Life-Changing Principles

Graham Warner

A Real Apprentice
Copyright © 2013 by Graham Warner
Accompanying discussion questions can be found at: www.grahamwarner.com

All rights reserved. No part of this book may be reproduced or transmitted in any form or by any means, electronic or mechanical, including photocopying and recording, or by any information storage and retrieval system, without permission in writing from the publisher.

Unless otherwise noted, all Scripture references are from, *The NEW AMERICAN STANDARD BIBLE®*. NASB®. Copyright © 1960,1962, 1963, 1968, 1971, 1972, 1973, 1975, 1977 by The Lockman Foundation. Used by permission.

Scripture quotes marked NIV are taken from the HOLY BIBLE, NEW INTERNATIONAL VERSION®. NIV® Copyright © 1973, 1978, 1984 by International Bible Society. Used by permission of Zondervan. All rights reserved.

Scripture quotations marked KJV are taken from the *Holy Bible, King James Version*.

Scripture quotations marked NKJV® are from the *New King James Version*. Copyright © 1982 by Thomas Nelson, Inc. Used by permission. All rights reserved.

Scripture quotations marked MSG are from *The Message*. Copyright © 1993, 1994, 1995, 1996, 2000, 2001, 2002. Used by permission of NavPress Publishing Group.

Cartoons by Graham Warner and Samuel Fogelqvist
Concept used by permission Scripture Union (John Pickering)

DEEP RIVER BOOKS
PO BOX 310
Sisters, Oregon
www.deepriverbooks.com

ISBN-13: 9781937756758
ISBN-10: 1937756750

Library of Congress: 2012952903

Cover Design by David Litwin, Purefusion Media

Contents

Introduction 13

101 Life-Changing Principles

1. Teach them to observe everything that I have 16
   commanded you (Matt. 28:18)
2. Sell your coat and buy a sword (Matt. 4:17; Mark 1:15) 18
3. Repent for the kingdom of heaven is at hand 20
   (Matt. 4:17; Mark 1:15)
4. Rejoice and be exceedingly glad, leap for joy 22
   (Matt. 5:12; Luke 6:23)
5. Let your light shine before men that they may see 24
   your good works (Matt. 5:16; Mark 4:21, Luke 8:16;
   Luke 11:33; Luke 12:35)
6. Leave your gift at the altar, but first be reconciled 26
   with your brother (Matt. 5:24)
7. Do not lust in your heart (Matt. 5:28) 28
8. You shouldn't divorce your wife (Matt. 5:32; 30
   Luke 19:9; Luke 16:18)
9. Let your yes be yes and your no be no (Matt. 5:37) 32
10. Turn the other cheek (Matt. 5:39; Luke 6:29) 34
11. If someone takes your shirt then give him your 36
    coat as well (Matt. 5:40; Luke 6:29)
12. Give to him who asks (Matt. 5:42) 38
13. Go the second mile (Matt. 5:41) 40
14. Love your enemies (Matt. 5:44; Luke 6:27, 35) 42
15. Bless those that curse you (Luke 6:28) 44
16. Be perfect as your Father in heaven is perfect (Matt. 5:48) .. 46
17. Ought to pray and not lose heart (Luke 18:1–8) 48
18. Don't practise your righteousness before people (Matt. 6:1) . 50
19. Fast in secret (Matt. 6:16-18; Luke 5:35) 52
20. Do not lay up treasure on earth (Matt. 6:19) 54
21. Do not be anxious for your life, what to eat 56
    or drink (Matt. 6:25; Luke 12:22, 29)

22.	Don't be ashamed of me or my words .... 58 (Matt. 10:32-33; Mark 8:38; Luke 9:26; 12:9)	
23.	If anyone does not hate father, mother, wife, ... 60 children…cannot be my disciple (Luke 14:26)	
24.	Take up your cross and follow me (Matt. 10:38) 62	
25.	Come to me all that labor and are heavy-laden .... 64 (Matt. 11:28)	
26.	He who has ears to hear let him hear (Matt. 11:15) 66	
27.	Seek first the kingdom of God (Matt. 6:33) 68	
28.	Do not judge or you will be judged (Matt. 7:1-2; John 7:24) 70	
29.	Be merciful as your Father in heaven is merciful .... 72 (Luke 6:36)	
30.	Take care what you hear (Mark 4:24) 74	
31.	Do not give what is holy to the dogs (Matt. 7:6) 76	
32.	Ask, seek and knock (Matt. 7:7; Luke 11:9; John 15:7, ... 78 16:24)	
33.	Have faith in God (Mark 11:22) 80	
34.	Ask the Father in my name (John 15:16; 16:23) 82	
35.	Treat others as you want to be treated (Matt. 7:12; .... 84 Luke 6:31)	
36.	Enter by the narrow gate (Matt. 7:13; Luke 13:24) 86	
37.	Beware of false prophets (Matt. 7:15) 88	
38.	Build your house on the rock (Matt. 7:24-27; Luke 6:47) ... 90	
39.	Much is required from all who have received much .... 92 (Luke 12:47–48)	
40.	Follow me (Luke 9:57-62; John 12:26; Luke 14:27) 94	
41.	I desire mercy and not sacrifice (Matt. 9:13; 12:7) 96	
42.	Don't put new wine into old wineskins (Matt. 9:17; .... 98 Mark 2:21-22; Luke 5:36-38)	
43.	Ask the Lord of Harvest to send out laborers .... 100 (Matt. 9:38; Luke 10:2)	
44.	Go and bear much fruit (John 15:1–8, 16) 102	
45.	Go, saying the kingdom of heaven is at hand ....104 (Matt. 10:7; Luke 10:9, 11)	
46.	Heal the sick (Matt. 10:8; Luke 9:2; Luke 10:9) 106	
47.	Raise the dead (Matt. 10:8) 108	

48.	Cast out demons (Matt. 10:8; Mark 16:17) 110
49.	Cleanse the lepers (Matt. 10:8) 112
50.	Do not hinder those casting out demons (Luke 9:50) 114
51.	Freely you have received, freely give (Matt. 10:8) 116
52.	Do not go from house to house (Mark 6:10; Luke 10:7) . . . 118
53.	As you enter a house give it your greeting of peace . . . . 120 (Matt. 10:13; Luke 10:4)
54.	Give a cup of cold water (Matt. 10:42) 122
55.	Shake the dust off your feet (Matt. 10:14; Mark 6:11; . . . . . 124 Luke 9:5)
56.	Be as wise as serpents and as harmless as doves . . . . 126 (Matt. 10:16)
57.	When they persecute you in this city flee to the next . . . . . 128 (Matt. 10:23)
58.	Come aside and rest a while (Mark 6:31) 130
59.	Either make the tree good and its fruit good, or . . . . 133 make it bad (Matt. 12:33)
60.	Behold, behold, behold, and behold! (Matt. 12:41, ... 135 42, 49–50; 13:3–8)
61.	Hear then the parable of the sower (Matt. 13:18) 136
62.	Honor your father and mother (Matt. 15:4–7; Mark 7:10) . 138
63.	Honor the Lord with the heart, not just lip service . . . . 140 (Matt. 15:8; Mark 7:6 Implied)
64.	Watch and beware of the leaven of the Pharisees . . . . 142 (Matt. 16:6; Mark 8:15; Luke 12:1)
65.	Whatever you bind on earth will be bound in heaven . . . . 144 (Matt. 16:19; Matt. 18:18)
66.	Become as a child (Matt. 18:3; Mark 10:15) 146
67.	Whoever receives a child receives me (Matt. 18:5; . . . . 148 Mark 9:37; Luke 9:48)
68.	If your hand or foot causes you to stumble, cut it off . . . . . 150 (Matt. 18:8; Mark 9:45; Luke 17:2)
69.	If your brother sins, reprove him (Matt. 18:15; Luke 17:3) 152
70.	If he repents, forgive him (Luke 17:3) 154
71.	Forgive up to seventy times seven . . . . 156 (Matt. 18:21; Luke 17:4)

72. If you wish to enter into life, keep the commandments . . . 158
    (Matt. 19:17; Luke 18:20)
73. Do not lord it over, whoever wishes to be great must 160
    serve (Matt. 20:26; Mark 10:43; Luke 12:26)
74. Render unto Caesar the things that are Caesar's 162
    (Matt. 22:21; Mark 12:17; Luke 20:25)
75. Love God with all your heart (Matt. 22:37; Mark 12:30; . . 164
    Luke 10:27)
76. Love the Lord your God with all your strength 166
    Matt. 22:37; Mark 12:30; Luke 10:27)
77. Love the Lord your God with all your mind (Matt. 22:37; . 168
    Mark 12:30; Luke 10:27)
78. Love your neighbor as yourself (Matt. 22:39; Mark 12:31) . 170
79. Go and do likewise (be a Good Samaritan!) (Luke 10:37) . 172
80. Do what they say, do not do what they do (Matt. 23:3) . . . 174
81. Do not be called teacher/father/leader (Matt. 23:8-10) 176
82. Don't neglect justice, mercy, and faithfulness (Matt. 23:23) 178
83. Do not be troubled by wars and rumours (Matt. 24:6; 180
    Mark 13:7; Luke 21:9)
84. Care for the poor and needy (Matt. 25:35–37) 182
85. Give what is in the plate as charity (Luke 11:41) 184
86. Take, eat, this is my body (Matt. 26:26; Mark 14:22; 186
    Luke 22:19; John 6:53)
87. Go into the world (Matt. 28:19) 188
88. Make disciples of all nations (Matt. 28:19) 190
89. Baptize them in the name of Father, Son, and Holy Spirit . . 192
    (Matt. 28:19)
90. Don't take the best seats (Luke 14:8) 194
91. Invite the poor, crippled, lame, and blind when you 195
    give a meal (Luke 14:13, 21)
92. Make friends by using money (Luke 16:9) 198
93. Don't say three months then harvest (John 4:35) 200
94. Wait until you receive power from on high (Luke 24:49) . . 202
95. Do not marvel, all in the tombs shall hear his voice 204
    (John 5:28)
96. Do not work for food that perishes (John 6:27) 206

97.	Abide in me and my words (John 8:31, 15:4)	208
98.	Walk in the light (John 12:35)	210
99.	Wash one another's feet (John 13:14, 15, 17)	212
100.	If you believe in God, believe also in me (John 14:1)	214
101.	Love one another (John 15:12, 17)	216
	All 303 Commands of Jesus in the Gospels	219
	Endnotes	233

Acknowledgments

I have to acknowledge a debt of gratitude to all those who have chiseled and sculpted my thinking through the years. Particular thanks to the churches and small groups that have been instrumental in the formulation of the discussion material which accompanies this book. (Hundreds of questions as discussion starters now available at www.grahamwarner.com).

Especial thanks to my remarkable wife, Kate, without whose help this book would never have reached its final form. I am grateful for her unfailing support and encouragement as we have sought to live out the principles contained in these pages.

I apologize to my readers in the United Kingdom for the Americanisms contained within, but nevertheless wish to express my gratitude to Deep River Books for their professionalism, diligence, and hard work in bringing this book to fruition.

INTRODUCTION

As the blinding angelic light continued to invade the darkened cell, manacles and chains jangled to the floor, and city lights beckoned through the open door. But this angel now demanded that Peter go back and preach in the very place of his recent arrest. Guess what? He went! What would you do if an angel appeared in your bedroom tonight? Would you respond with equal blind obedience? Actually, you would be crazy not to. When a supernatural being puts in an appearance, it is usually of great consequence. Angelic visitations brought essential guidance throughout the Old and New Testaments: Mary and Joseph for example, were given help with their first Christmas arrangements; Peter was "aided and abetted" in this great escape from prison—twice! Paul was instructed how to "abandon ship" after his fourteen-day Titanic experience with a storm. Angels gave clear instructions which were to be followed to the letter. Hebrews 2:2 states that "The word spoken through angels proved unalterable." If we are to be held accountable for carrying out the commands of an angel, how much more important must it be to carry out the instructions given to us by the Son of God? Hebrews 2:1 declares, "For this reason we must pay much closer attention to what we have heard, lest we drift away from it."

The significance of the commands of Jesus cannot be underestimated. His words were not just "off the cuff" comments, but were calculated, premeditated directives from God. They were thought through in heaven and handed to Jesus by his Father. Jesus affirmed, "I do not speak on my own initiative, but the Father himself who sent me has given me a commandment, what to say, and what to speak.... Therefore the things I speak, I speak just as the father has told me" (John 12:49, John

---

The teaching of Jesus places greater emphasis on how we should behave than on what we should believe;
This is a 'whole life system,' not just a 'belief system.'

17:8). A true disciple then, should hang on his every word. A major part of his earthly mission was to give the world his commands. He is therefore a true "Commander"—not a title often associated with Jesus. Not only did he command the attention of great crowds but also imparted commands that revealed masterly insights into divine and human nature. He presented a blueprint for our mental health and happiness and set out a radical manifesto for crafting a better society. As a compilation, his commands also constitute a supremely challenging life manual. Jesus's words have changed history and transformed millions of devoted followers. Some say his teaching is open to interpretation—but actually his challenges are unmistakably straightforward. This book sets out to demonstrate that Jesus calls a spade a spade: he means what he says and says what he means. The trouble is we sometimes don't like what we hear! His words penetrate like well-driven nails, and whatever area of life is under his hammer, he hits each nail squarely on the head. Interestingly, his teaching places greater emphasis on how we should behave than on what we should believe—in other words he promotes a *whole life system* not just a *belief system*.

The Commander rightly questions, "Why do you call me 'Lord, Lord,' yet do not do what I say?" (Luke 6:46–47).

A Real Apprentice

1

Teach them to observe everything that I have commanded you

MATTHEW 28:20

Famous last words! At least these are some of them, recorded right at the end of the Gospels in what is known as The Great Commission. We will start at the end because here Jesus sums up the core of what it means to be a disciple. He had, by now, finished his whole teaching program, and just before he ascended back to heaven he gave one last exhortation: He said "Make disciples" i.e. learners or *apprentices*, "teaching them to *observe everything* that I have commanded you" (Matt. 28:18 emphasis added). A cycle started that day that was to repeat itself with each subsequent generation. What Jesus had taught his disciples was to be passed on to each new generation of converts. We then have the same challenge today as they had in the first century—to seek to obey *all* the commands of Jesus and teach others to do the same. These pages cover one hundred and one thought-provoking principles from the teaching of Jesus about the definitive characteristics of a real apprentice.

> His teaching began to change everything about me.

Although I was raised in church circles, strangely, the words of Jesus were never presented to me as imperative, or even serious. If I am really honest, belief in Jesus seemed little more than an acceptance of his dying on the cross as our way of salvation. Granted, Jesus was a brilliant storyteller and I loved his stories, but many of them seemed to have little bearing on modern life with references to slaves, sheep, sowing, and such like. The impression I was given was that his death was the only really significant issue in the Gospels. So, when I read through all four

Gospels at the age of nineteen, I remember being astonished by what I was reading. How could I have been in church all my short life and missed this?

The more I read his challenges, the more amazed I became, and the more my desire grew to become a genuine follower of Jesus. His teaching began to change everything about me: my lifestyle, my personality, my theology, my job, my ambitions, my relationships—everything!

Jesus's principles provide the keys for anyone to discover personal transformation. The more I studied them however, the less resemblance I could see to modern Christianity. How crazy is that? Why didn't the church teach me that to follow Jesus meant exactly that—to follow Jesus, lock, stock, and barrel? Sadly, I am not alone in my experience, for there seems to be very little emphasis on the commands and words of Jesus in modern discipleship training. I have often asked in churches how many commands Jesus gave us. The normal response is just two! Actually, there are three hundred and three commands, or implied commands, in the Gospels, so these 101 points are just a taster. I hope this will encourage you to dig deeper to see if you can discover the remaining two-thirds. (Actually we will cover most of them as we go along, and they are all listed for you at the end of the book). This book seeks to put Christ back into "Christ"-ianity!

A Real Apprentice   17

> *Field full of treasure, take the surface or top treasure, or we can dig to get that which is of real worth.*

2

Sell your coat and buy a sword

LUKE 22:36

"Let him who has no sword sell his robe and buy one!" This strange and rather controversial command highlights one of the dilemmas in writing this book: not only do we need to understand the original intention of Jesus's statements, but also to work out if their application is for disciples of all generations, i.e. forever commands. There are, of course, a number of Jesus's commands (thirty-one that I can find) which were applicable to a "one off" situation in his earthly life two thousand years ago, so, we need to sift and sort his commands to discover those that require twenty-first-century action. For example, when Jesus instructs his disciples to "Go into the village and bring back a colt," the only colt we are likely to find today would be a Mitsubishi car, or even worse—a gun! Or the command, "Rise, take up your bed," could lead us to presume that Christians should carry their beds each day once they have gotten up. And when Jesus says, "Buy a sword," what are we to do?

If we were to link the phrase "buy a sword" with "compel them to come in," we would have a recipe for the Crusades! Conversions forced by the sword was clearly not what Jesus intended! Or were we to link the *buy a sword* to the statement, "if your hand offends you, cut it off," we would have an equally objectionable practice. This is, of course, used by some religious fanatics who remove hands, and even heads, in some

18   Graham Warner

parts of the world! (It is important to note that, if necessary, Jesus's command states that we amputate *our own* limbs, not those of other people. But don't worry; there will be further clarification on how to do this later!)

> If necessary, we amputate our own limbs, not those of other people.

I confess I don't understand why Jesus suggested purchasing a sword. Was it to prepare the disciples for being alone for the first time (Jesus was about to leave but the Spirit had not yet come), or was it perhaps symbolic of spiritual warfare? Fight the good fight and all that! Or was this sword merely for use as a deterrent, as some use the nuclear argument today? Personally, I would prefer to believe that it was for use in food preparation such as spreading butter on apostolic toast! Jesus certainly wasn't suggesting here that his disciples literally fight for the kingdom, for when Peter did use a sword Jesus had to rectify the damaged slice of ear! He also warned that, "those who take up the sword would perish by the sword" (Matt. 26:52), and later added that his servants would not fight because his kingdom was not of this world (John 18:36). Incidentally, I did once purchase a sword (so that I could at least tick off this command as done) but hasten to add that I have never used it, not even in the kitchen! But in general, I don't think this command applies to us today—I'll let you decide! Interestingly, the disciples never did this, because strangely they already had two swords and Jesus said, "It is enough!" (Luke 22:38)

Be led + taught by the Spirit
Jesus is the same yesterday, today & forever.
Therefore's God's Word same, doesn't change, so dig to find treasure, even in unlikely places

3

Repent for the kingdom of heaven is at hand

MATTHEW 4:17; MARK 1:15

"Repentance" is the first identifiable command of Jesus, which is unfortunate, in that this rather old-fashioned word possesses negative religious overtones. However, it simply refers to change. Change can be positive, and for Jesus that is the name of the game. His commands demand change from every new apprentice. His principles are so radically different from anything we would do by nature that every would-be disciple must actively decide to realign himself in order to follow. His commands define heavenly values, which more often than not present a wisdom which is the very antithesis of worldly wisdom. (For example, the world sees nothing wise about turning the other cheek! But we will later discover the amazing heavenly wisdom in this). Because Jesus's commands seem to be diametrically opposite to worldly ways, to embrace them demands a 180 degree change in thinking and direction.

To repent is frequently described as a U-turn, but I prefer to think of it as a "you-turn" because it involves a personal commitment to turn towards Jesus. This is more than merely turning away from wrongdoing—it is demonstrating that relating to Jesus is key to this change, and that he is now the new focus. The Old Testament Ten Commandments were also relationship based, i.e. not just a list of rules. For example, the first four were about relating to God: "You shall have no other Gods before me," etc. So too, the commands of Jesus are not just a list of cold, unrelated rules, but perfectly define how we can relate to the Son of God. In him we also see these rules being worked out in practice. He asks nothing from us that he himself does not already do. The incentive for living by these heavenly rules is that Jesus draws close to those who obey them. Hence the rest of this statement—"the kingdom of heaven is at hand." This is a phrase we shall encounter again later, but *at hand* literally means so close we can reach out our hands and touch it. This isn't change for change's sake! It is change that opens the door for heaven to touch our lives! Following the commands of Jesus is an adventure into change. His words reach into every sphere of human experience, and give us solid ground on which to stand.

"Whoever hears these sayings of Mine, and does them, I will liken him to a wise man who built his house on the rock" (Matt. 7:24 NKJV).

This isn't change for change's sake!
It is change that opens the door for heaven to touch our lives!

4

Rejoice and leap for joy

MATTHEW 5:12; LUKE 6:23

Jesus, we are told, was anointed with joy above his companions, so it is quite clear that he really enjoyed life. It would be fun to see his extreme kind of joy touching earth a little more often. Jesus had much to say about joy. For example, he promised to give his joy to his followers, and further explained how this joy could be made full. Amazingly, the context of the most extreme form of joy in the Gospels is persecution. "Blessed are you when men hate you, and ostracize you, and cast insults at you, and spurn your name as evil, for the sake of the Son of Man. *"Be glad* in that day and *leap for joy,"* Luke 6:22–23 (emphasis added). What a contrast between worldly, natural reactions and heavenly joy, for no human being would naturally enjoy persecution!

Matthew's account uses the expression "be *exceedingly* glad." This is no mild form of joy. When was the last time that you were so elated that you literally jumped for joy? Is it my spirit of heaviness, or the weight of responsibility that I carry, or am I just plain too heavy? I don't seem to do much jumping! My personal leaping for joy is usually goal orientated, but unfortunately the soccer team that I support doesn't score many! If it were the winning goal, the Christmas bonus, some miraculous healing,

---

Amazingly, the context of the most extreme form of joy in the Gospels is persecution.

---

or a dramatic conversion, I could understand such an expression of jumping joy. However, this instruction is given in the context of intense trials and tribulations.

Rejoicing is the last of eight "beatitudes" in Matthew chapter 5, of which the other seven are also beautiful attitudes, such as humility, selflessness, purity of heart, peacemaking, etc. Each beatitude describes a personal attitude in which we should *be*, (i.e. "Be-Attitudes"). Extreme joy is the climax of this list, but to be honest, I am not sure how we obey this. Can we genuinely turn on joy when adverse circumstances prevail? The answer has to be—yes! Given that we are full of the Holy Spirit, the fruits of the Spirit such as love, *joy,* and peace constantly bubble up from within. An old adage says, "If your cup is full of sweetness, no matter how hard you are jogged, you will not spill a drop of bitter water." May all your jogs today be full of joys!

5

Let your light shine that they may see your good works
MATTHEW 5:16; MARK 4:21; LUKE 8:16; LUKE 11:33; LUKE 12:35

This is also an interesting command—notice that its primary focus is the light, not the good works. What is this light? When history's artists tried to depict holy people and saints of the past, they would often paint a golden halo around their heads. I have always dismissed this as religiosity, but perhaps these characters actually did emit some kind of radiance. Do you remember singing in Sunday School, "This little light of mine, I'm gonna let it shine"[1]? I don't think I ever understood to what the candle referred! Interestingly, one rather rude, cynical criticism levelled at me recently was, "Light shines out of his backside!" How ironically complimentary! I wonder how those artists would have depicted that particular halo?

Paul wrote in 2 Corinthians 4:6, "For God, who said, "Light shall shine out of darkness," is the One who has shone in our hearts to give the Light of the knowledge of the glory of God in the face of Christ." So, just as God caused light to shine into the darkness of creation at the beginning, he now speaks into being the same light in us. Jesus spoke of a time when "The righteous will shine forth as the sun in the kingdom of their Father" (Matt. 13:43). It seems that we will shine with full radiance one day. Believe it or not, that light is shining

> "The righteous will shine forth as the sun
> in the kingdom of the Father."

now, although veiled by the flesh, and so Jesus encourages us not to hide it under a bucket, or a bed, or in the cellar, for we are the light of the world!" (Matt. 5:14–16),

So what exactly is this light? Well it is Jesus of course, for he is the light of the world and now he is living in us. Jesus is described as the radiance of God's glory (Heb. 1:3). This radiance illuminates God at work through him. Those who observed the miracles of Jesus gave praise to God the Father, not to Jesus, because they were aware of this supernatural dynamic. Hence this command for us: "Let your light shine before men in such a way that they may see your good works, and glorify your Father who is in heaven" (Matt. 5:16). There is something about this light shining on our good works that leads observers to thank God, rather than us, for our deeds! We need to ask one another, just like cigarette smokers do, "Have you got a light?"

6

Leave your gift at the altar, but first be reconciled with your brother

MATTHEW 5:24

Here is another command from the Sermon on the Mount. It makes three important observations. Firstly, it is important to note the distinction between the offender and the offended. We are not being asked here to consider if we have been offended by a brother—for when someone offends or hurts us, we must learn to forgive and forget. (We will look at how to find this kind of forgiveness a little later.) No, this command is not giving us permission to air our grievances with others. Rather, it requires us to consider if we are guilty of *causing* offense or hurt to another, and if so we must be proactive in making amends. Jesus said, "Make friends quickly with your opponent at law while you are with him on the way, so that your opponent may not hand you over to the judge, and the judge to the officer, and you be thrown into prison" (v 25). There's no question here as to who is the guilty party!

Secondly, the Lord is highlighting the importance of right relationships. The question, "Have I upset anyone, anywhere?" is sufficiently important to the Lord that everything be put on hold until any issues are resolved. I am not convinced that we will always find the harmony we desire with everyone. The apostle Paul wisely commented that *as far as it is possible,* we should be at peace with all men. The very nature of persecution, as predicted by Jesus, means that we will occasionally cause offense to some, who will not be appeased. However, Jesus does require that we play our part in doing all that we can to live in harmony and reconciliation. This should of course be accomplishable with *everybody* in the church!!

> The question to ask is 'Have I upset anyone anywhere?'

Thirdly, the emphasis here is on speed. One might expect Jesus to order us to go home along with our gift, only to return with it once reconciliation has occurred. But instead, he requires that we leave our gift at the altar *whilst* we resolve matters. Now, if that offering were a lamb, it would need securing at the altar, implying that our remedial actions must be undertaken swiftly and instantly. We often take so long to respond to issues that the lamb would have become mutton or even died of old age before we returned to offer it as a sacrifice! The moral of this point is—if you need to be reconciled to someone today—do it now!

7

Do not lust in your heart

MATTHEW 5:28

I was once told that lust is only like window shopping or reading the menu outside a restaurant—permissible provided that we are not tempted. So can we use the retort "just looking" when it comes to appreciating members of the opposite sex?

"You have heard that it was said do not commit adultery but I say to you that everyone who looks at a woman to lust for her has committed adultery with her already in his heart" (Matt. 5:27-28). Good news for single people! Presumably, single people can lust after single people, because there can be no issue of adultery! Unfortunately not, as with much of Jesus's teaching, he is here giving us a miniature snapshot from which we gain wisdom to apply to *all* similar situations. Sorry about this, singles, it is possible that this also applies to you! Nor should we reason that if, having lusted after someone (and therefore, according to the text, are already guilty of adultery), that we may just as well sleep together anyway, for the battle is already lost. Certainly not! The outward act must be a more serious sin, as it is sin both against society and even against one's own body (see 1 Cor. 6:15–18).

Probably most men have committed mental adultery at some time or other, and maybe some women too (although my wife thinks women are more likely to lust after a pair of shoes than another man). Jesus was highlighting what the Ten Commandments had already told us: "You shall not covet your neighbor's house; you shall not covet your neighbor's wife" (Exod. 20:17). Actually, the Greek word for "covet" in the Greek translation of the Old Testament is apparently the same word that Jesus used for "lust." So the concept of being accountable for our internal desires was the culmination of the Old Testament Law, i.e. the tenth and final commandment. Jesus narrows the focus and uses lusting after a woman as his example, but he could equally have used the other examples of coveting from the Ten Commandments. "You shall not covet your neighbor's house; you shall not covet your neighbor's wife or his male servant or his female servant or his ox or his donkey or anything that belongs to your neighbor." Desiring status is probably a modern equivalent to the "servants", the "ox" could equate to someone's job; the "donkey" to someone's car, or any of their possessions in general. Coveting is a strong internal desire to "have." It is where internal hungers drive us. I am tempted to add chocolate, alcohol, food in general, and of course that pair of shoes! Jesus compels us to clean up our inner world, whether that is our emotions with anger or hatred, or our thought life with lust. Sin is conceived in our hearts, or minds, long before it gives birth to an outward expression. Playing with fire usually ends with somebody getting burned!

> Playing with fire usually ends with somebody getting burned.

8

You shouldn't divorce your wife

MATTHEW 5:32; LUKE 19:9; LUKE 16:18

Divorces seemed to have been a common experience in Jesus's time both among the Jews and the Greeks, and sadly, affect almost one in two marriages today! So this command is as relevant now as then, and although it constitutes a rock of offense to many, nevertheless, we can understand the important place marriage has as the building block for family and society. Having personally been through, not a divorce, but a marriage annulment, I can understand the pain many go through struggling with Jesus's words here, as well as the agony of broken relationships.

We need to note that Jesus does allow divorce with what is known as the "exception clause," variously translated *except for the cause of fornication/unfaithfulness/adultery/indecency*. The context is Jesus answering a direct question from the Pharisees about a passage in Deuteronomy 24:1. "Is it lawful for a man to divorce his wife for *any cause* at all?" (Matt. 19:3 emphasis added). In Jewish and Greek society, it was apparently commonplace and legal to divorce your wife for "any cause," such as burning the toast, for example! Jesus here clearly opposes their practices, emphasizing that marriage is intended to be lifelong. However, there are legitimate exceptions, e.g. sexual intercourse with another person, which potentially breaks the marriage bond (just as intercourse consummated the marriage bond in the first instance).

There is also a hint of divorce in Exodus 21:10–11, which cites neglect as a possible reason. This pertains to the neglect of essential materials as well as conjugal rights, which could be construed as physical and emotional abuse. However, the context here doesn't fit well in a Christian/Western culture, as it refers to the taking of an additional wife!!

Apart from these exceptions, which could define irretrievable breakdown, Jesus is clearly against divorce. Marriage is intended to be lifelong—for better, for worse, for richer, for poorer, in sickness, and in health, and so on. Rather than looking for excuses to end a marriage, Jesus expects us to realign and readjust in order to live together in harmony, practising forgiveness and reconciliation. "The two shall become one flesh." Perhaps this refers to the mystical union, and also perhaps to the children born of that union, and for both of their sakes—"What God has joined together, let no man separate."

> Rather than looking for excuses to end a marriage, realign and readjust in order to live together in harmony, practicing forgiveness and reconciliation.

9

Let your yes be yes and your no be no
MATTHEW 5:37

From broken marriage vows, Jesus now moves on to broken promises—say what you mean and mean what you say. Jesus demands that we be people of our word, always known for speaking the truth. When we say yes it means yes, and when we say no it means no. How many times have you heard the use of expressions like, "Cross my heart and hope to die!" or "I swear on the life of my children" (perhaps "mother-in-law" would be a more popular option!)? Interestingly, Jesus comments that anything beyond the statement of truth to enhance the truth is actually evil (v 37). So, ironically, the very statements we make to emphasize how right we are, such as "honest to God," actually exposes our unrighteousness. "Anything more than this is evil."

> 'Do according to all that proceeds out of your mouth.'
> Always remain true to your words.

There are two issues in focus in the context of this expression. One is oaths and the other is vows. Jesus says, "Do not swear at all: neither by heaven…nor by the earth…nor by Jerusalem" (Matt. 5:34–35 NKJV). Nowadays, we are more familiar with swearing an oath on the Bible, involving a promise to speak the truth while laying a hand on the Good Book. Uttering an untruth thereafter would then be invoking punishment from God, so the assumption is that only the truth will be spoken. Ironically, it is those who don't take the Bible seriously who swear on it in court, because those who take its message seriously don't!

Jesus quotes what "the ancients" were told in Leviticus 19:12 (presumably, referring to the Jews in ancient time, not the very old people of today!). They were not to make false vows using God's name. This, the Law says, profanes his name. So these old people would make their oaths using the names of earth or heaven instead of God's name. But Jesus reminds us that earth and heaven also belong to God, so the Lord's name is still profaned—albeit indirectly. So, don't swear by anything—just tell the truth, at all times.

Numbers 30:2 says, "If a man makes a vow to the Lord, or takes an oath to bind himself with a binding obligation, he shall not violate his word; he shall do according to all that proceeds out of his mouth." The Law required that any vow made to the Lord must be fulfilled, and any promise accomplished. Jesus further emphasizes that honoring promises made to people (be it a neighbor, children, or spouse) is as important as honoring those made to God. In the words of Numbers 30:2, "Do according to all that proceeds out of your mouth." Always remain true to your words.

Turn the other cheek

MATTHEW 5:39; LUKE 6:29

Here Jesus recognized an obvious fact of life—everyone suffers hurt from time to time. It is a matter of *when,* not *if.* The wisdom of his response, however, is less obvious, "Whoever slaps you on your right cheek, turn to him the other also" (Matt. 5:39). My personal philosophy would be "When someone is about to strike you—duck!" And if they try to strike the other cheek—double the duck! Can there be any sense in offering our back to persecutors? Why does Jesus say, "Do not resist him who is evil"?

Many of us would prefer the Old Testament policy of an eye for an eye and a tooth for a tooth, hand for hand, foot for foot, burn for burn, wound for wound, bruise for bruise (Exod. 21:24–25). Having grown up with three brothers I am no stranger to the principle of *give as good as you get.* Retaliation seemed the only way people (e.g. brothers) might learn to respect me! But revenge is never as simple as "give as good as you get" (i.e. like for like). In all probability, the reality is more likely to be "worse for like"; for example an "If you poke my eye out, I'll kill you" scenario. Of course, the Old Testament policy attempted to address this very issue by proposing a damage limitation strategy, so that any reaction was to be limited to like for like. So the Old Testament was not advocating taking revenge—quite the opposite. Self-control was to be exercised—a feature likely to be lacking from a natural worldly response. But Jesus goes a step further by dismissing the concept of retaliation altogether.

Take a look at the news. Vengeance does not solve the problem of aggression. Violence just begets more violence. Jesus's response shows his genius—we should absorb the initial pain, and then turn the other cheek, the wisdom being that the second cheek will invariably escape being struck. Absorbing the initial blow—without retaliation—will more often than not diffuse the matter and bring it to a swift end.

> Do not resist him who is evil.

During the course of my work I have been physically attacked eleven times. Three times I have been threatened with knives; once (rather oddly) someone was attempting to stab me in the forehead. On another occasion I was knocked unconscious by an enraged youth—a very peaceful experience for me! On that occasion the opportunity of turning the other cheek never arose, unless he struck me again while I was out cold! However, on all eleven occasions, I can honestly say that in the heat of the moment, the Holy Spirit has absorbed my own aggressive reflex.

Jesus took the taunts, the whip, the punches, and the nails without retaliating. In fact forgiveness was his only form of retaliation. It is only with his help, and his Holy Spirit living in us, that we can bless those who curse us and do good to those who spitefully use us (Luke 6:28).

11

When they steal your shirt give your coat as well

MATTHEW 5:40; LUKE 6:29

Giving to someone who is stealing from us may seem a little foolish. Certainly it would be tantamount to encouraging a criminal in his life of crime. Surely our task as Christians is to educate this thief regarding rights and wrongs, and the law dictates that he be punished. Worldly wisdom would judge the principle of blessing a robber to be totally crazy—and yet Jesus finishes the Sermon on the Mount (where our title statement is to be found) with the understanding that it is a wise man who hears his sayings and does them (Matt. 7:24). Actually, embodied in this seemingly mad idea is a stroke of genius, which serves to highlight the dramatic difference between two kingdoms: This is where the best in the kingdom of God engages with the worst in the kingdom of the world—and emerges triumphant!

There are three reasons why this is kingdom wisdom of the highest order. Firstly, it provides a coping mechanism for us when a thief breaks in and steals. (Jesus astutely warns this will occur as often as moth and rust destroy.) Unfortunately, it is one of those unpleasant facts of life that will affect us all at some stage. A burglar once broke into my flat in London but couldn't find anything worth stealing—how embarrassing! The only item he took was a suitcase to help him carry away the spoils from a neighboring flat. So giving the shirt off my back, or at least something extra as Jesus suggests here, was difficult when he wanted nothing of mine in the first place. On other occasions I have had items of sentimental, rather than monetary value stolen—that's painful! The world has no answer for this pain, but Jesus gave us the key to heal bitterness and unlock forgiveness—this key is quite simply generosity! It's not just the willingness to let go of possessions, but the desire to overcome the abuse by giving something extra, which turns the situation around—the thief is now not taking from me…I am giving to him!

Secondly, it gives value to people whom (let's face it) everybody hates. In fact thieves probably even hate themselves, being aware that they are social parasites. But Jesus came to demonstrate that seemingly worthless people have value and are worthy of sacrifice. We need to show love and respect to them, irrespective of their unsociable behavior. Yes, of course we need laws, law courts, and police. The law of the land is the same law that potentially leads people to Christ. But when sinners encounter Christians, they should experience a taste of grace. We exercise mercy because we have received great mercy.

Finally, this also tests where our treasure really is—as to whether our hearts are in the material world or the spiritual. Rather like this next principle!

> "It is a wise man who hears these sayings and does them."

12

Give to him who asks

MATTHEW 5:42

Luke quotes Jesus as saying "Give to everyone who asks." Ouch! This also hits where it hurts. He then goes even further by adding "lend, expecting nothing in return" (Luke 6:30–35). Materialists and the wealthy will clearly not find this Jesus philosophy very palatable! Live like this and we will have nothing left! Or will we? Actually we can never out-give God—he says, "Give, and it will be given to you; good measure, pressed down, shaken together, and running over" (Luke 6:38). God requires us to give because he himself gives—very generously! It is one thing to give to those who ask, but quite another to actively say, "Ask of me and I will give you whatever you ask." Yet that is the essence of prayer—a generous God who is willing to give in response to our requests. Incidentally, the wisdom on the subject of lending is quite interesting—most people who borrow something will never return it. So if this were the expectation, there would be no disappointment! How wise is that? However, there is no suggestion that we should refuse to accept items back if returned. The hope is that this will not happen.

The word for *gift* in Greek is "charis," which also translates as "grace." I don't have any doubt that giving releases grace into people's lives. Giving blesses people, but also releases God's grace to them. When we give in the physical realm, something happens in the spiritual sphere. I could cite many miracles, healings, and conversions which have resulted from simple acts of giving. Maybe there are times when we must say, as Peter did, "Silver and gold have I none" but grace still has something to give—

> "Lend, expecting nothing back."

such as a blessing of healing. You may be familiar with the quip about the lame man "who asked for alms and got legs."

In the Old Testament, the Law provided various means for the poor: Farmers were to leave the edges of their fields unharvested for their provision. Olives and grapes were to be reaped just once per season with the remaining growth left for the poor. These and other laws required people to lay aside something for those in need. Not a bad concept for us to emulate—that we lay aside a small financial sum each week to meet any needs which may be brought to our attention. Then we wouldn't be troubled by someone stopping us on the street to ask for some change. Perhaps this fund should also be used to cover stolen items and "the extras" we give, from our last point—a kind of "Give to him who asks" insurance policy!

13

Go the second mile

MATTHEW 5:41

An interesting Roman law permitted a soldier to commandeer someone to carry his bags for one mile, and this was undoubtedly common practice in occupied Palestine. Once approached, the victim would have been obliged to carry out this duty. One can imagine the crowds scurrying away from any soldier with bags under his arms. But after Jesus had instructed his followers to "go the second mile," I guess disciples would have proactively approached soldiers to offer their services. This would have been frustrating for the soldier if he were only a mile from home, because he would have found his luggage a mile beyond his destination! I jest.

> I am glad we have a God who goes the second mile.

Actually, this is a brilliant life principle. It sets a new standard for our attitude towards our daily duties and gives us renewed incentive to work. Everyday tasks become a form of worship, because we are now serving Jesus, not the Romans! The boring and mundane turn into valuable expressions of love, for Jesus said, "If you love me, you keep my commandments" (John 14:15). Imagine being in the shoes of a Roman soldier—you would no doubt be accustomed to resentment and verbal abuse from your conscripted bag carriers. You may have even developed a guilt complex about the oppression you create. Suddenly your stuff-bearers become happy and willing conscripts. These Christians' joyful spirits seem to energize them as they walk through the streets undoubtedly singing Graham Kendrick's song, "Make way, make way!"[2] Wow, what an impact!

To go the second mile doesn't necessarily mean putting in twice as much time. It is possible to double productivity in the same time. I think that Christians should be able to work twice as hard as non-Christians, partly because it is fun to use everyday activities as an expression of our faith, but also because we can run on the energy which God supplies. "They that wait upon the LORD shall renew *their* strength; they shall mount up with wings as eagles; they shall run, and not be weary; *and* they shall walk, and not faint." (Isa. 40:31 KJV). I am glad we have a God who goes the second mile with us, always willing to do abundantly more than we ask or think (Eph. 3:20)—a God who equips us by the Spirit to do the same.

A Christian has a brilliant incentive to do more than he is asked. Thank God for the hidden agenda, that even if our service is never noticed nor acknowledged by our bosses, it is nevertheless noticed by the Lord, and thus becomes a high form of worship.

14

Love your enemies
MATTHEW 5:44; LUKE 6:27, 35

Jesus gave his life for us while we were unlovable sinners. Even though we had rejected God, he still thought we were worth dying for. In the same way, Jesus calls us to love the unlovable. "You have heard that it was said, 'You shall love your neighbor and hate your enemy,' but I say to you 'Love your enemies'" (Matt. 5:43 NKJV). In verse 46, Jesus goes on to say that if you love those who love you there is no reward, because even the tax-gatherers do that. What then makes us different from the tax gatherers? (Sorry, tax gatherers, it's not my analogy. I would have used the Traffic Wardens!) The answer is that we love the unlovable, even our enemies (including tax collectors and Traffic Wardens!).

I learned the lesson about loving the unlovable in a very graphic way, while looking after homeless teenagers in London. A homeless young man, who came to live with us, turned out to be totally objectionable. His language was foul, abusive, and rude. He was, we later discovered, regularly mugging elderly people. On just one court appearance, he was charged with stealing thirty-eight cars. Basically, he was not very nice! Actually, my stomach would turn over when he entered the room. He opposed everything we—an extended family—stood for, and we eventually came to the conclusion that he would have to go. I spent an entire day contacting hostels and reception centers, but he had already been thrown out of them all, and none were willing to have him back. I quite understood, but that didn't solve my problem.

By the end of the day I had become totally frustrated. That night as I prayed, I blurted out, more honestly than I had intended, "Lord, I hate him!" But in doing so, I suddenly became aware that the Holy Spirit had begun to pray through me. "I hate him, but I know you love him. I don't understand how or why you love him but would you love him through me?" By the time I rose from my knees, I experienced an intense love burning within, so strong that I fasted for the next seven days for him, and my instant desire was to spend time with him. When he became a Christian, his life changed radically, so much so that his probation officer commented that it was just as though he had "turned from darkness to light." Interesting terminology from a non-Christian! But the real miracle was that God changed me. He showed me that my human love was inadequate for this kind of situation (in fact, in any kind of situation), and

> This love is not dependent on the person we are trying to love, neither is it dependent upon us, but upon God—who is love!

that I needed to love with "agape" love. I needed Jesus's love in my life. This love is not dependent on the person we are trying to love, neither is it dependent upon us, but upon God—who is love!

15

Bless those that curse you

LUKE 6:28

As far as Jesus is concerned, loving your enemies is more than just a sentimental, fuzzy feeling. It is a tough determination to exercise kindness in the face of your enemy's adversity. "Do good to those who hate you, bless those who curse you, and pray for those who mistreat you" (Luke 6:27–28). The new challenge is to overcome evil with good, to be bigger than our opponents by maintaining the moral high ground. As light overcomes darkness so blessing overcomes cursing, goodness is greater than hatred, and we pray to release good things to those who would mistreat us. It is easy to glibly say, "Bless you," when someone is rude but quite another to actually desire and pray for the very best to happen for them. That is blessing in the face of cursing!

This naturally follows the last principle (loving one's enemies) for it demonstrates that Jesus type *agape* love is practical in nature. It requires a definitive expression in order to exist. Agape love is the result of choice whereas *phileo* love (Greek for "natural love") doesn't need an expression; it is merely a sentiment or a feeling over which we have no control. Phileo love is automatic. It simply happens and does not require expression.

> Do not be overcome by evil, but overcome evil with good.

So we can love the girl next door with Phileo love without ever revealing it. Agape, however, involves a deliberate decision, selecting the object of our love and the method by which we shall express that love. Jesus suggests that we seek blessing for, do good to, and pray for the people who are the most undeserving of it in our lives.

Romans 12:20–21 demonstrates the practical nature of this blessing. "If your enemy is hungry, feed him, and if he is thirsty, give him a drink; for in so doing you will heap burning coals upon his head. Do not be overcome by evil, but overcome evil with good." Incidentally, it has been suggested that heaping burning coals on someone's head was indeed a blessing not a curse for the delayed revenge of hellfire. In historic Jewish culture if an enemy's fire died, it would have been customary to provide him with a burning coal[3], so that he could rekindle his fire (no cigarette lighters in those days!). To provide him with many coals—in fact an entire fire—would indeed have been a blessing, and this he would have carried in a tray upon his head. I have always preferred this interpretation rather than the idea that blessing an enemy now will result in him burning a little hotter in hell later.

16

Be perfect as your Father in heaven is perfect

MATTHEW 5:48

I love the way that this appears at the end of this chapter almost as a casual afterthought. By the way, be perfect! I once spoke at a University Christian Union meeting where a student walked out in protest because I had admitted my own imperfection. He considered it a waste of time to listen to someone who was not perfect. That was a few years ago, and the shocking thing is that I am still struggling with imperfections! Sorry, you may not want to read any further...

Actually, the more I meditate on the principles of Jesus the more imperfect I feel. They set an incredibly high standard which contrasts with the way I naturally think and live. Nevertheless, because each principle is perfect within itself, amassing them together must surely define total perfection. I have always loved these words of Jesus, no matter how crazy they may seem, because my heart—the very core of my being—knows them to be absolutely right and true. The problem is how to live by them!

The simple answer is that we cannot fulfil these commands in our own strength. Only Jesus can do it. They are expressions of his nature, not ours. He alone can consistently react and behave like this. We love Jesus so much that we want to imitate him. So, the solution is for us to ask Jesus to live out his principles in us and through us. Then we can effectively "be" Jesus in society. "It is no longer I who live, but Christ who lives in me; and the life which I now live in the flesh I live by faith in the Son of God, who loved me and gave Himself up for me" (Gal. 2:20 NKJV).

> It is no longer I who live, but Christ who lives in me.

If Jesus lives his life again in us, then we become transformed to his nature, as Matthew 5:45 says, "In order that you may be sons of your Father in heaven." His commands are expressions of his nature, which explains why he can, for example, love his enemies. This love hinges upon his loving nature, not the person receiving this love, however unlovable they may be. Hence he causes the sun to rise on the evil and the good, and sends rain on the righteous and the unrighteous.

Of course, there is another way that Jesus makes us perfect and that is in our standing before God. We are made as those justified from our sins. Justified—"Just as if I'd" never sinned. Hallelujah! Believing in the fact that Christ died for our sins can free us totally from every stain and every blot. Everyone has the right to be forgiven and cleansed because of the perfect work accomplished on the cross.

17

Pray and do not lose heart

LUKE 18:1–8

It is not known how much time Jesus spent alone in fellowship with his Father; however, there are certain clues. For example, we read that on one occasion he rose a great while before day, and when he took a stroll walking on the water in the fourth watch of the night (that was somewhere between 3.00 and 6.00 a.m.), he had spent that night up until then in prayer. He did the same thing before choosing the twelve disciples (i.e. spent the night in prayer, not the walking on water bit!), and of course prayed more earnestly than any man in the Garden of Gethsemane. Not surprisingly, Jesus taught us much about prayer. We are instructed to pray and not lose heart (Luke 18:1-8).

Amazingly, in all his teaching, Jesus never once entertained the prospect of prayer remaining unanswered. Everything he said was gloriously positive. "Ask and you shall receive"; "Ask the Father anything in my name and he will give it to you"; "Ask believing that you will receive and you shall have whatever you are asking for." There is no mention of a maybe or a might, not even a wait. Did you notice—"you *shall* have," "he *will* give," "you *will* receive"? Admittedly our experience is often not so. I can only presume it is not God's fault. His intention is that prayer works! Unfortunately, our mistake is that we often neglect the conditions which accompany the encouragements.

I have compiled a list of the twelve conditions given to us in the New Testament regarding prayer. In the event of an unanswered prayer I use this checklist, rather like a diagnostic chart, and usually identify my error. Here are some of the things Jesus says in the Gospels: Ask in Jesus's name (John 15:16); ask believing; ask without doubting (Mark 11:23–24); don't pray with vain repetitions (Matt. 6:7); don't pray like the hypocrites (Matt. 6:8); pray in this way—like what we call the Lord's prayer (Matt. 6:9–13); pray with a forgiving spirit (Matt. 6:14–15); pray and keep on praying, and do not lose heart (Luke 18:1).

Compare it to a motor vehicle—the engine will function if the appropriate mechanical requirements are met. If it falters, something needs changing. Maybe it's time to service our prayer lives and get on the road! Prayerlessness limits what God is able to do. I personally believe that God channels all that he does through the prayers of his saints. Let us pray!

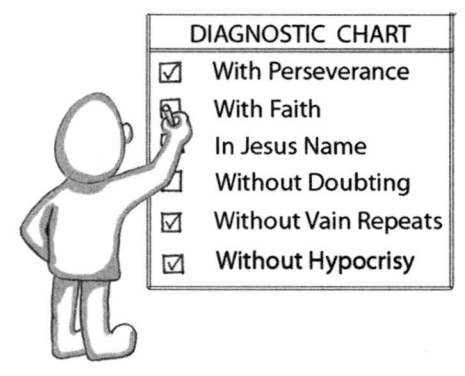

DIAGNOSTIC CHART
- ☑ With Perseverance
- ☑ With Faith
- ☑ In Jesus Name
- ☑ Without Doubting
- ☑ Without Vain Repeats
- ☑ Without Hypocrisy

> Jesus never once entertained the prospect of prayer remaining unanswered.

18

Don't practise your righteousness before people
MATTHEW 6:1

Jesus now apparently contradicts his earlier statement where he encouraged us to let our light shine before men. Here he requires that we keep our righteousness secret. For instance, it is acceptable to publicly bless those that curse us, but religious duties like giving, fasting, and praying should be done privately. The hypocrites liked to stand on street corners praying. They would also attract attention to their giving into the temple treasury, and donned sackcloth and ashes to manifest the hardship endured while fasting, but probably never went the second mile to help somebody or ever gave away a coat in response to the theft of a jacket!

The actions of the hypocrites revealed their seriously inappropriate motivation, doing things to be seen of men. To impress and gain honor resulted in their missing the benefits of God's reward. As Jesus pointed out, they had already received their reward from men. They were respected and revered from a human perspective, and their reward was therefore complete, period! But when we hide our righteousness, then the God who sees in secret will reward us openly. So when you give—don't let your left hand know what your right hand is doing (Matt. 6:3). Shut the door and pray in secret. Put on a brave face and continue as normal so that your fasting goes unnoticed. Secrecy is the secret that is admired and blessed by God!

A tree, I believe, has as much surface area below the ground as above it. These hidden roots give the tree strength. Its roots grow deeper in times of drought thereby increasing its strength. Our strength, too, is dependent upon the hidden side of our lives, as we develop our roots deeper into the Lord. We know Jesus spent time alone with his Father, but interestingly we don't know the details of how much time he spent in prayer, or fasting, or how much he and his disciples gave to the poor. These things still remain a secret. Paul took fourteen years before disclosing that he had been caught up into the third heaven, where he heard things that were not lawful to be heard. Eventually he shared the experience, but he never shared the details of what he had heard there. These were special, private, and secret, and gave him his hidden strength. I have become more and more convinced as a preacher that God doesn't reward the act of preaching. It is so difficult to preach in secret! No, it is not the preaching he rewards but the prayer, fasting, and secret seeking God's face behind the scenes. This is a wonderful leveller between those with public and those with more private ministries. It is everything done in secret that counts in God's eyes!

> When we hide our righteousness, the God who sees in secret will reward us openly.

19

Fast in secret

MATTHEW 6:16–18; LUKE 5:35

"Fast" is so inaptly named, because every fast seems to go so slowly! Should we call it a slow? "When you fast, anoint your head and wash your face, so that you may not be seen fasting by men." Notice that Jesus assumed that fasting would be part of our discipleship, by saying *when* not *if*. Apparently, the Pharisees fasted every Monday and Wednesday, and Jesus expected that our righteousness would exceed that of the Pharisees (Matt. 5:20). Jesus started his ministry with a forty-day fast, but we have no record of his fasting agenda thereafter. Perhaps he fasted the same days as the Pharisees, or perhaps he had no regular fast days. He lived by his own principles and maintained secrecy! We know that there were times when he was too busy to even eat (Mark 6:31), which is in itself a kind of fast—fasting to work rather than fasting to pray.

The children of Israel fasted from wearing jewelry.

Jesus explained in John 4:34 that his food was to do the will of the Father and to accomplish his work. He apparently refused the food obtained for him by the disciples. We also know that he fasted from sleep, which is another valid form of fasting. In fact, I really enjoy sleeplessness, for such is the pace of life that it is only the night hours which provide me with real quality time with the Lord. There are many ways to fast. A total food and drink fast is one example, or perhaps a partial fast from certain kinds of foods, such as rich or sweet, or from meats (like Daniel). Paul speaks of husbands and wives fasting from sex in order to give themselves to prayer. Single folks are presumably fasting in this area anyway! The Sabbath was a fast from work, to take time out to be with the Lord. The list is probably endless. How about a television fast? A colleague of mine once fasted from crossing his legs. He was praying for someone who was unable to do so. Whenever the desire to cross his legs occurred, my friend was prompted to pray for his healing. The children of Israel fasted from wearing jewelry after the incident of the golden calf. They also fasted from homely comforts for seven days annually, in a celebration called the Festival of Booths, where they would live for an entire week in shacks made from branches! The Nazarites fasted from cutting their hair and from drinking strong alcoholic beverages. Well, there's plenty of scope for the imagination. Go for it! Be creative! Enjoy!

20

Do not lay up treasure on earth

MATTHEW 6:19

When Jesus speaks about money I become uncomfortable! He probably has more to say about wealth and riches than any other topic. On one occasion I worked through Luke's gospel with a red highlighter pen, marking every passage that made reference to money or material things. This was to be the subject of my next teaching session, and I decided instead of teaching to just read aloud through these passages. There is a wealth of material in most chapters. On arrival at the meeting, I realized that I had made a massive mistake. My Bible has all the words of Jesus printed in red. My red highlighter exercise had neatly rendered invisible everything I had marked! I now have a valid excuse to ignore some of these difficult passages. You may want to do the same with your Bible!

Seriously, Jesus has a message we need to hear in our materialistic society where success is measured in pounds and pence. Prosperity is even the measure of spiritual success in some areas of the church. I won't knock it—it just doesn't seem to work that way for me! Money definitely seems to attract some "spiritual health warnings." For example: Don't lay up treasures upon earth (Matt. 6:19); Beware against every form of greed, (Luke 12:15); You can't serve God and money (Matt. 6:24; Luke 6:13); The rich he sends away empty-handed (Luke 1:53); The deceitfulness of riches chokes the Word (Luke 8:14); Where your treasure is there will your heart be also (Matt. 6:21); What is a man profited if he gains the whole world (Luke 9:25); Render to Caesar what is Caesar's (Matt.

22:21), etc. Jesus rebuked a very successful business man, who intended building some bigger warehouses—"You fool! This night your soul is required of you" (Luke 12:20). "And so is the man who lays up treasure for himself, and is not rich toward God" (v 21). Now do you understand what I mean about that red highlighter?!

> He probably has more to say about wealth and riches than any other topic.

The real proof of the pudding is to ascertain how Jesus lived. Did he, I wonder, own anything more than the clothes in which he stood? "Foxes have holes, and the birds of the air have nests, but the Son of Man has nowhere to lay his head" (Luke 9:58). He encouraged his disciples to carry no purse (Luke 10:4), and suggested that any potential follower should deny himself and take up his cross (Luke 9:23).

So long as we understand Jesus's warnings regarding the dangers of riches, he does also give us the other side of the coin. For example, he commends those trading with talents and doubling their money, and told of successful farming stories, and created supernatural catches for those in the fishing business! Give and it shall be given back to us in pretty good measure!

21

Do not be anxious for your life, what to eat or drink
MATTHEW 6:25; LUKE 12:22, 29

Switching on the television is sufficient to raise anxiety levels. Terrorism abounds here, there, and everywhere! Lawlessness seems to have ascended to new levels of atrocity. Documentaries like "Seconds from Disaster" and "Air Crash Investigation" demonstrate the fragility of life, and natural disasters sweep away thousands of innocent people in literally seconds. Yes, worry is part of living in the modern world. But once again Jesus had the antidote. His message was simple, appropriate, and relevant—*don't be anxious!* The Bible apparently repeats the instruction to *fear not* 366 times, one for every day of the year and one extra for the leap year. In fact, this is the most commonly occurring command in Scripture. Let us consider three things Jesus said about anxiety:

Firstly, don't be anxious about your life (Matt. 6:25). "Worrying will not add a single cubit to your life's span," in fact quite the opposite—it could considerably shorten it. He told us not to worry about what we are going to eat or drink, or what

> The Bible repeats the instruction to 'fear not' 366 times, one for every day of the year and one extra for leap year

we are going to wear. Jesus said, "Life is about more than food or clothing!" Trust God our heavenly Father to look after us for all our daily

56   Graham Warner

needs. The birds of the air don't sow or gather into barns, yet are supplied for. If God does this for the birds, how much more would he do that for us? It is an interesting observation that birds never store their food. They live hand to mouth, or is it foot to beak? Yet the next meal is always forthcoming.

Secondly, don't be anxious about tomorrow (Matt. 6:34) for tomorrow will take care of itself, each day has enough trouble of its own. Probably 95 percent of the things which cause us concern never happen—so why worry about them? Unfortunately, I spend 95 percent of my time worrying about the remaining 5 percent of things that do happen! I am joking! Psalm 118:5–9 is a great passage to calm our fears: "If the Lord is for me; I will not fear." Fear oppresses us and squeezes us into a corner, but the Lord rescues us and sets us in a large place. Incidentally, verse 8 is the middle verse in the whole Bible. It says, "It is better to trust in the Lord than to trust in man." What an excellent core message!

The third and final area is, don't be anxious about what to say (Matt. 10:19–20. Even here the Father supplies for our needs. He will speak through us, hence....

22

Don't be ashamed of me or my words

MATTHEW 10:32–33; MARK 8:38; LUKE 9:26; 12:9

We need not be anxious about what to say, for Jesus promises to provide the right words when we need them. That is comforting! However, he continues by saying that our words will bring a sword, and will cause even family members to become enemies; brother will deliver up brother to death, and a father his child, and children will rise up against parents, causing them to be put to death. We will be hated by all on account of his name, but we must not fear those that kill the body! Well, that is reassuring!!

Actually, I am so very proud of Jesus and his words. I am sure you agree. So, why is it that we sometimes experience embarrassment when confronted by certain people in certain situations? Peter experienced this. He boldly asserted that he would rather die than forsake the Lord then went through a trilogy of denials. This kind of experience must be common to all his followers otherwise these words of Jesus would be irrelevant. The fact is his words are so contrary to the way the world thinks that we are destined to find ourselves at variance with the worldly. Our comments are very likely to go against the grain. Hence, "Do not think I came to bring peace but a sword," Matthew 10:34. And that unfortu-

> "Everyone who shall confess me before men, I will also confess him before my Father who is in heaven."

nately sets "a man against his father, and a daughter against her mother, and a daughter-in-law against her mother-in-law." Oops!

Jesus continued, "Everyone who shall confess me before men, I will also confess him before my Father who is in heaven." In other words, he will be proud of us if we are proud of him. The alternative is unthinkable, however—"If you deny me I will also deny you." I have never been certain of the implications of this. Could Jesus stop interceding for us, or does he cease to be our advocate before the Father? I don't know! And for sure I don't want to find out! "Lord, give me boldness to proudly stand for you, and strength to follow your words whatever the consequences."

23

Hate father, mother, wife, children...
LUKE 14:26

At last, we find a command that is easy to follow and comes quite naturally. Alright, I am joking! Actually, this is more of an observation than a command, but I allocate this to the category of *implied* commands. It is impossible to be a disciple without hating your family members. This seems somewhat strange and at odds with his whole message of love. I hasten to add that husbands are the only ones exempt from this list. Sorry, wives! You are going to have to continue to love your men!

It doesn't include husbands

The context here is the same as our previous point—family members may hate a disciple because of his allegiance to Jesus. This raises the question of compromise. Does loyalty to family come before devotion to Jesus? "He who loves father or mother more than Me is not worthy of Me" (Matt. 10:37). By the way, only God could demand such love, so this makes an interesting statement when applied to Jesus. He demands a loving devotion that is only fitting for Divinity.

> Does loyalty to family come before devotion to Jesus?

It is commonly understood that the "hatred" defined in this passage is only hatred in comparison to the love we have for the Lord. This is, nevertheless, a powerfully shocking principle, and seems to challenge much of modern teaching on the priority of the family. For the twelve disciples, suddenly called away from their businesses and homes to pursue Jesus's evangelistic campaign, these verses were particularly poignant. Jesus himself knew that pursuing the road to the cross would pierce through his own mother's heart like a sword. It's not that he didn't care. As he was dying on the cross, Jesus delegated the care of his mother to John, thus proving his concern. But his agenda is a bigger issue and demands such sacrifices for the cause.

Jesus compounds the shock of this command by adding that a disciple should hate even his own life. I don't think I have ever heard a sermon about hating oneself. I have heard many times that we should love ourselves. After all, it is difficult to observe the command to love my neighbor as myself if I don't love myself. But Jesus seems to be emphasizing the very opposite—"Hate your life!" We will look at this again later but I introduce it now as a tease! Suffice it to say that I have never really loved myself very much, so I find these words strangely comforting. More on this later!

I should add that when our priorities are correct, love is our Christian duty towards all people, even family members! Particularly when they make themselves our enemies!

24

Take up your cross and follow me
MATTHEW 10:38

"Take up your cross" is an amazing statement, the significance of which could be easily missed. Yes, this does refer to the challenge of making sacrifices as we follow Christ. At the same time, however, we discover this amazing prophetic statement concerning crucifixion! Each of us can predict that we will die. That is inevitable. It is not so easy, however, to say how it will happen. But Jesus predicts how he will die, his burial and resurrection, not just once, but thirty-seven times before the event. He similarly predicts the "church" long before it came into being in Matthew 16 and 18, when for example he says, "Upon this rock will I build my church." Brilliant! The predictions concerning his death include expressions such as he would "be lifted up," just as Moses lifted up a brass serpent in the wilderness. Also that he would be buried for three days, as was Jonah in the belly of a fish. Parables such as the son and heir being killed by the stewards whilst visiting his vineyard also spoke of his own fate. Furthermore he made many open and clear references to his suffering, dying, and rising again three days later. The mention of the *cross* here was a clear foresight of his earthly demise!

> 'He is no fool who gives what he cannot keep, to gain that which he cannot lose.'

"Take up *your* cross" means that we too each have a cross to bear, hereby predicting our potential suffering which can be directly attributable to our discipleship. The cross speaks of self-denial—our death to selfishness. Excuse the pun, but it is a *crossroad*—a choice between living for ourselves or dying to ourselves. This is summed up in Christ's prayer—"yet not as I will, but as *You* will" (Matt. 26:39 emphasis added). I have often used an acrostic on the five letters in "cross" which defines how we might suffer as we follow Christ; these come from Matthew 10. "C" is for **c**riticism—"If they called the head of the house Beelzebub, how much more the members of his house?" (v 25). "R" stands for **r**ejection—"You will be hated by all on account of my name" (v 22). "O" is for **o**pposition—"They will deliver you up to the courts and scourge you" (v 17). "S" warns us of **s**atanic attack—"I send you out as sheep in the midst of wolves" (v 16). And the final "S" is for **s**acrifice—"He who has lost his life for my sake shall find it" (v 39).

Actually, it isn't really a sacrifice to give up everything for Jesus, because in losing life we find it. As the martyr Jim Elliot once said, "It is no fool who gives what he cannot keep, to gain that which he cannot lose."[4] The question I need to ask myself is "Have I lost my life?" Paul reckoned that anything that was gain to him was lost to Christ, and he counted all things to be loss in view of the surpassing value of knowing Christ (Phil. 3:7-10). What have I lost in the pursuit of Christ, or is everything as it would have been were I not following Jesus?

A Real Apprentice   63

25

Come to me all that labor and are heavy-laden

MATTHEW 11:28

A cross is not the only item we must carry; we must also carry a yoke. This is the yoke given to us by Jesus and he describes it as "easy" and its burden "light." These extremely popular verses refer to more than just heavily pregnant women (those in labor), or those of a particular political persuasion (those in the Labor Party); they invite *all* who labor and are heavy-laden to off-load personal burdens and weariness in exchange for rest. How burdened and weary does the journey through these 101 commands of Jesus leave you? Only seventy-six more to wrestle with! The children of Israel had to wrestle with just Ten Commandments (actually there were 613 in total). I have deliberately used the word *w-rest-le*? Note the position of the word rest! The notion here is that we experience rest in the midst of our labor, as we effortlessly birth these concepts. Believe it or not, this yoke is easy. Why? Because the yoke is not ours, it is the yoke of Jesus. Hence, "Take *my* yoke upon you" (emphasis added).

The apostle Paul warns against being unequally yoked. But if we are sharing a yoke with Jesus, the inequality of the partnership could not be greater. Imagine a huge animal yoked with a tiny one, such as an elephant yoked with a husky dog. The elephant would clearly handle the workload, while the husky's feet would probably not even touch the ground. And so it is being yoked with Jesus; the partnership is so unbalanced as to render us totally insignificant. Jesus not only shoulders the work but also carries us in the process.

Appropriately, there is a second command in connection with this yoke. That is, "Learn from Me, for I am gentle and humble in heart." When a number of horses are harnessed together, they will follow the lead of the dominant animal, and thereby learn submission. Jesus invites us to be harnessed to him for similar purposes. We discover as much about the nature of the one to whom we are yoked as about the work

> *Wrestle*? Note the position of the word rest! The notion here is that we experience rest in the midst of our labor.

and the direction of travel. It is his gentleness and humility which facilitate such an agreeable pairing with one so overwhelmingly powerful. Imagine being yoked to an overbearing, arrogant personality—that could be unbearable and certainly hard work! But in this relationship we find rest for our souls and a sense of ease, we settle back and enjoy the ride. "I will give you rest," he promises. His gentleness would not break off a battered reed, or extinguish a smouldering wick. *Rest* is God's promise in Hebrews 4:9—"There remains therefore a...rest for the people of God." "Let us therefore be diligent to enter that rest" (v 11).

26

He who has ears to hear let him hear

MATTHEW 11:15

Jesus taught in parables not only to make his message simple and memorable, but also to conceal the message from the spiritually unaware. Those on the same wavelength as Jesus understood, but others completely misunderstood. Isaiah foretold, "Their eyes see but they do not perceive, their ears hear but they do not understand" (Isa. 6:9–10). The disciples should have been as attuned to the true message as a radio to a certain frequency. Truth is not just heard, but is spiritually discerned, revealed through the Holy Spirit. Jesus taught by faith, expecting his Father to reveal the meaning to his listeners. He rarely interpreted his parables, so comprehension would remain elusive unless the Father and the Holy Spirit provided enlightenment.

So, this principle pertains to the spiritually sensitive, with ears sufficiently acute to hear. Six times in the Gospels Jesus repeats, "Those who have ears to hear let him hear." On each occasion, a secret revelation is available only to those with receptive antennae. Why not put this to the test and see whether you have ears to hear? The six passages are as follows:

1) John was the greatest, but the least in the kingdom is greater than he. (Matt. 11:15)
2) The man who hears brings forth fruit, 30 fold, 60 fold, and 100 fold. (Matt. 13:11–23)
3) The righteous will shine as the sun in the kingdom. (Matt. 13:43)
4) There is nothing hidden/secret that will not be revealed. (Mark 4:22–23)
5) The things which come out of man are what defile the man. (Mark 7:15–16)

6) If salt has become tasteless it is useless, and thrown out. (Luke 14:34–35)

These statements are deliberately cryptic to encourage further reading and meditation. Study the Bible passages and ask the Lord for revelation. See what happens. Go on, try it now!

Jesus once asked, in essence, "Who do people say that I am?" Peter in that moment recognized that he was the Christ. "Blessed are you," Jesus said, "because flesh and blood did not reveal this to you, but My Father who is in heaven." Revelation is supernatural! So, "If you have ears to hear then hear," and develop this wonderful gift!

> "You are blessed," Jesus said, "because flesh and blood did not reveal this to you, but my Father who is in heaven."

Seek first the kingdom of God

MATTHEW 6:33

Of all the words of Jesus, this verse has challenged me the most. It has been my lifetime favorite and the verse upon which my entire ministry has been built. This verse spoke powerfully to me as a naïve twenty year old and motivated me to live by faith as a full-time Christian worker. I embarked on an unpaid career of evangelism simply trusting that God would provide for my everyday needs. That is the amazing promise connected to this command—seek first the kingdom of God and his righteousness and he will add everything else that we need. When I started out in Christian work, I was unbearably naïve (a characteristic unfortunately lost through the years) and launched out, not quite knowing how things would turn out. My premise was that if the Lord didn't supply for my needs, I had about forty days in which to serve him before I starved to death. After all, had he failed to feed me, the worst that could have happened would be the best thing that could happen—I would have died and gone to heaven!

But miraculously he did supply for my every need, and has continued to do so throughout my life. I was young then, but although I am now fifty-something and grey haired, these words remain just as true as they ever did. I must admit that there have been many occasions when I have not known where the next meal would come from, or how the next bill would be paid: but the Lord has never failed to provide.

The key is just to continue to seek his kingdom and his righteousness! The greater my needs became, the greater the anticipation of a miracle grew—and those miracles consistently happen.

> "For he who comes to God must believe that he is, and that he is a rewarder of those that seek him."

Our lives are not our own, we belong to the Lord. I believe he enjoys working out how to take care of us. Our responsibility is to seek God's interests, and he in turn seeks our interests. Time doesn't permit me to relate the stories or share the testimonies of how our needs were met. But I once bumped into a complete stranger on the street and he gave me his car! He couldn't have known that I had been praying for a vehicle for some evangelistic work just ten minutes earlier, with my Bible open at this very verse. The most wonderful testimony is his—not how my needs were met, but how he supplied for someone else's need, quite supernaturally! He had been feeling he should give his car away; as I bumped into him he felt the Lord say "this is the man."

Seeking his righteousness means following the do's and don'ts of Jesus the King. Each page in this book seeks to describe what is meant by his righteousness. Surprisingly, Jesus's righteousness is more about do's than don'ts. People often get a negative idea about Christianity. Actually, Jesus gave us only nineteen don'ts out of our 101 commands, so Christianity is mostly summed up by eighty-two do's!

28

Do not judge or you will be judged

MATTHEW 7:1–2; JOHN 7:24

Having said this, we now consider one of those rare don'ts—"Don't judge." It is not that we should never make judgments, for we obviously need to discern between rights and wrongs. When evaluating a person's character, for example, we need to be able to make some kind of judgment about the fruits in his or her life. And how can we remove a speck of dust from our brother's eye if we are unable to recognize its presence? (Of course we are expected to remove the logs from our own eyes first!) And how can we admonish one another without first making some form of critical observation? Yes, judgments are necessary but seem to be categorised into *good* or *bad*—presumably dependent upon the motive driving them. If judgment entails putting people down, writing them off, criticizing, or even thinking negatively of them, then it is clearly destructive. The other side of the coin is demonstrated by Jesus, who came into the world not to judge it but to save it. It has been said, "The difference between condemnation and conviction is revealed within the words themselves!" Condemnation contains the word *damnation*, whereas conviction contains *victory*. In other words, good judgment tries to help and salvage a person, whereas, bad judgment tends towards character assassination.

> Condemnation contains the word 'damnation,'
> whereas conviction contains 'victory'.

There is clear incentive for not judging others, for we will also be judged should we do so. It seems God uses our own measure of judgment with which to judge us. If we pardon others, we will be pardoned (Luke 6:37). If we condemn, we will be condemned (Luke 6:37). It is unnerving to think that my pointing the finger forms the basis for God pointing his finger towards me. He uses exactly the same measure of judgment on me that I use on others. We are all amazed at the steward's reaction when, newly released from an enormous debt, he virtually killed someone who owed him a fiver; and yet that's often just how we behave (Matt. 18:22–35). Remember the incident in 2 Samuel 12:1–7 when King David heard a parable from Nathan, the man of God, concerning a rich man with a great many flocks, who took a poor neighbor's only lamb (like a pet to him) and had it slaughtered for a meal? David's anger burned greatly against this man and he said, "Surely the man who has done this deserves to die. He must make restitution for the lamb fourfold, because he did this thing and had no compassion." Nathan replied, "You are that man!" Suddenly, the light dawned for King David! We are too quick to judge others, yet so unwilling to judge ourselves! Well, in God's economy—we get what we give!

A Real Apprentice

29

Be merciful as your Father in heaven is merciful

LUKE 6:36

To *be merciful* means what it says—to "be full of mercy"! This is not just partial mercy for some, but wholehearted mercy for all, and Jesus cites our Father in heaven as our perfect example. He is described as "compassionate, gracious, slow to anger, abounding in loving kindness and truth; who keeps loving kindness for thousands, who forgives iniquity, transgression and sin" (Exod. 34:6–7).

> To 'be merciful' means what it says—
> to be full of mercy!

The unforgiving steward, and the incident with King David (from our last point) have relevance here too. The unforgiving servant had received great mercy, in that his massive debt of some ten thousand talents had been cancelled. But he had learned nothing of how to replicate similar mercy to someone who had wronged him just a little—an unpaid bill of just a hundred denari (Matt. 18:22–35). When his master heard about this travesty, his forgiveness was withdrawn, and the unforgiving steward was thrown into prison until he had repaid the debt in full! How vital it is, then, to demonstrate the same mercy towards others as we have received from the Lord. The question raised here is, could the forgiveness we have received from the Lord be withdrawn as a result of failure to show mercy to others?

King David was still to discover the extent of God's mercy. He himself had shown no mercy toward Uriah, Bathsheba's husband, and was harshly critical of the rich man in Nathan's parable (2 Sam. 12:1–7). But prior to this incident, David had always been a man of mercy—he twice spared Saul's life against popular expectation. Perhaps that explained God's mercy to David even when he had failed.

"Blessed are the merciful, for they shall receive mercy" is a beatitude running in parallel with the last principle concerning judgment. Mercy is substituting judgment with leniency, but equally could describe the exercise of pity and care for those in need of help. So mercy is also seeking to alleviate distress via kindness, charity, and blessing flowing from a heart of compassion. Even when we don't have massive injustices to forgive, we can still find areas in which to exercise a full measure of mercy.

30

Take care what you hear

MARK 4:24

At another time Jesus observed that it is not what enters into a man that defiles him, but that which proceeds out of him. Lust, adultery, murder, etc. proceed out of the heart. He was really making the point that foods in themselves don't defile. But there are other ways in which we open doors to allow our hearts to be tainted and defiled by that which enters. The gateways are the eye and the ear.

When I was at junior school I was once berated by a teacher who unfairly (I thought) singled me out in a class and accused me of being a vacuum cleaner. He remarked that I went about sucking up any rubbish available. The comment clearly hurt, for I remember it as though it were yesterday! Although I fail to recall the nature of the rubbish to which he referred—it obviously wasn't his geography lesson! I think Jesus was making a similar point. We can absorb huge amounts of rubbish; what we see and hear are bound to influence our hearts. Be mindful!

Much of what we hear is beyond our control. For instance, words that wounded us in our youth (which perhaps contained an element of truth) may have affected our personalities, perhaps shaping or even permanently damaging us. That's why I look rather like a Hoover! Sometimes we still listen to inner voices from the past speaking untruths, and they still influence, perhaps paralyze, or even control us. Listen to the

Graham Warner

words of Jesus because by them, he says, we are made clean. His words have power to change us for the better. His positive messages of truth can set us free, truly free! (See John 8:36.)

> Our minds and spirits are sensitive and need to be bolstered with positive, uplifting, edifying words of encouragement.

Some of what we hear, however, we can control. I refer not just to television and radio programs, or music to which we listen. It is the conversations we have, the questions we ask, the gossip we overhear, the criticisms we attune to, the lies and cutting comments we believe—even the negative inner voices which discourage and depress. Be careful what you hear! The heart is precious and must be guarded. Our minds and spirits are sensitive and need to be bolstered with positive, uplifting, edifying words of encouragement. Words really are powerful. They are capable of destroying in an instant or releasing and creating the most wonderful, life-changing, miraculous blessing!

31

Do not give what is holy to the dogs

MATTHEW 7:6

This follows on from the last principle, which was to take care what you hear. This warns us to take care what we say and to whom we say it. Don't cast your pearls before swine, for they will trample the pearls underfoot before turning to attack you. Perhaps Jesus is making reference to literal pigs and dogs that obviously have no appreciation of the finer things in life, as to what is holy or valuable. More likely, Jesus is adopting humorous picture language to refer to certain categories of people. I am sure some individuals will immediately spring to your mind! Yes, even church seems to have its share of these so-called pigs and dogs! Ok, perhaps not your church then!

The longer your walk with the Lord, the more pearls of wisdom and holy nuggets you acquire. Perhaps they could be scriptural revelations, or perhaps personal miracles, or healings. Whatever they may be, they are of great personal value and are particularly precious because they represent your personal encounters with the living God and form the foundation of your faith. If you were to share these precious experiences with a cynic, or with someone with a differing theological stance, not only could your pearls be trampled on but you could also feel personally attacked in the process.

Jesus refused to commit himself to certain individuals, for he knew what was in them; in other words, he couldn't trust them (John 2:24–25). We need to be able to read people sufficiently accurately to establish whether they would value the treasures we would share. Jesus gave a beautiful picture—that we should be as scribes who bring out of our treasury things both new and old (Matt. 13:52). What a lovely description of our storehouse of godly encounters and experiences! We seek to share these treasures to thrill and excite those whom we meet. Fellowship is the mutual sharing of personal treasures, and evangelism is the distribution of these jewels of the kingdom. Jesus challenges us with the exer-

> The longer you walk with the Lord, the
> more pearls of wisdom and holy nuggets you acquire.

cise of deciding which jewels and treasures to share with whom. Beware of the dogs and swine with no appetite for appreciation. Perhaps there was an element of this principle at work when, rather unusually, Jesus instructed some people he had just healed—"Don't tell anybody what I have done for you." The healing was to be a personal blessing between the Lord and themselves, and Jesus sought to spare them the indignity of being ground under some foot or other!

Ask, Seek, and Knock

MATTHEW 7:7–11; LUKE 11:9–13; JOHN 15:7, 16:24

Asking, seeking, and knocking could represent separate instructions, and could be listed as three different commands; but more likely, from the context, they represent one command regarding prayer consisting of three progressive stages. In the passages to which we refer Jesus states; "Or what man is there among you who, when his son asks for a loaf, will give him a stone? Or if he asks for a fish, he will not give him a snake, will he? If you then, being evil, know how to give good gifts to your children, how much more will your Father who is in heaven give what is good to those who ask Him!" There is a clear expectancy here that the Father gives—so ask! And if you do so, you will receive!

The only requirement here seems to be that of perseverance. Jesus himself is encouraging us to persist. Each phrase apparently uses the present continuous tense, and so could read: ask and keep on asking, seek and keep on seeking, knock and keep on knocking. If we do this the outcome will be gloriously positive. It *shall* be given, he who seeks *shall* find, and the door *shall* be opened. There are no ifs, buts, or maybes, but a threefold *shall*. As mentioned previously, Jesus never entertained the idea that prayer would ever remain unanswered. So emphatic is he that he repeats himself. Note this repetition! It is a technique Jesus uses whenever double emphasis is required (for example—"Truly, truly"). The verses in both Matthew and Luke contain this repetitive pattern: "Ask and it shall be given to you; seek, and you shall find; knock, and it shall be opened to you. For everyone who asks, receives; and he who seeks, finds; and to him who knocks it shall be opened" (Luke 11:9–10).

Everyone who asks receives! Everyone who seeks finds!

Note also—this principle is fully inclusive, for it states "everyone." *Everyone* who asks receives! *Everyone* who seeks finds!

Seeking progresses from asking. What are we seeking here? Is it the answer to our asking that we seek, or is it God's face? Jesus often quoted from the Old Testament Law; Deuteronomy 4:29 states, "Seek the Lord your God, and you will find Him if you search for Him with all your heart and all your soul." To make life a little more fun, God sometimes engages us in a game of hide-and-seek. Like any loving parent, he hides in an obvious place where he will easily be found, then enjoys the excitement on our faces in the moment of discovery! Come on, it's fun to seek, and even greater fun to find him! But what if there is no answer, no surprise discovery? What if heaven seems as brass as though the Lord is not at home? Well, he is home! Knock a little harder and the door will be opened to you. Actually the door is always open (Rev. 4:1), but it is always polite to knock before we enter!

Have faith in God

MARK 11:22

Faith is one of the conditions that go alongside successful asking, seeking, and knocking. When you ask, believe that you are going to receive and it shall be granted to you. In fact Jesus describes perfect faith here as believing that you have already received. That's the kind of faith God displayed in creation, when he spoke and everything that is now came into being. By faith the worlds were framed" (Heb. 11:3). I am not a Greek scholar, but I am told this phrase, "have faith *in* God" should read "have faith *of* God." There seems a world of difference between those two statements. If the faith I exercise is actually God's faith, not mine, I can understand how Jesus could infer that you can speak to a mountain and say be taken up and cast into the sea, and it would happen.

> The trouble with being double-minded is that you can only ever be half-hearted.

Mind you, I am glad that Christians don't do that too much. Imagine how many holidays would be ruined by Christians moving the landscape around. You would have to listen to the latest geography bulletin to see where the Peak District is today! Of course if you didn't approve of yesterday's rearranging of mountains, you could always put them back today! I have always been amused at Adrian Plas's idea of practising these skills on a paperclip first! Joking aside, when it comes to moving mountains, I don't have any doubt that Jesus could do it, and doubt, or the lack of it, seems to be part of the issue here.

Jesus describes the successful mountain mover as the one who believes and does not doubt in his heart. Our English word for doubt comes from the Latin word *dubitare*, from which we get our word "double." James 1:6-8 defines a man who has doubts as double-minded. The trouble with being double-minded is that you can only ever be half-hearted. You see, faith is one mind and unbelief is one mind—doubt is a bit of both! Jesus is encouraging us to have faith, and to have faith means to exercise faith!

That's fine if we have faith. I have had non-Christians say to me, "I wish I had your faith," as though somehow we have it or we don't. Here Jesus is inspiring faith in all, so it is for all. Faith is being convinced of something. I like the definition that I've used in sermons for many years: "faith is an intelligent stand based on reason." Are we really convinced in God's ability to answer prayer? When we are convinced, faith follows automatically! I have often used the illustration that faith is like the action of sitting down. If we were not utterly convinced of the chair's ability to support our weight we would not sit on it. So being convinced precedes our action of faith.

34

Ask the Father in my Name

JOHN 15:16; 16:23

As mentioned earlier, Jesus provides us with strategies for effective prayer. Here is another one of them... we should pray *in the name of Jesus*. Is this some kind of secret formula which miraculously allows God to hear us when we attach it to the end of prayer? Or is it a polite way of signing off, rather like using "yours sincerely" at the end of a letter—to alert the Lord that we have now finished? No! It is actually the authority by which we pray, and the motivation behind our petitions.

The Lord began his prayer with "hallowed be thy name" (Hallowed, not Harold as some child mistakenly thought was God's name). Perhaps it would flavor our prayers considerably were we to start with the phrase, "in the name of Jesus," for we would need to ascertain if our prayers were about to revere his name. Jesus always glorifies the Father as the Father always glorifies the Son. Herein lies our reason for praying too—to glorify Jesus. John 16:3 states that the Father answers by giving us whatever we ask, *in Jesus's name*.

This then, is God's motivation—he responds for Jesus's sake. The passage continues, "ask, and you will receive, that your joy may be made full." Joy in itself is not often considered to be a motivation for prayer, but when our joy becomes full because Jesus is being glorified, we are certainly on the right track!

"You shall not take the name of the Lord your God in vain" is one of the Ten Commandments of the Old Testament. Respect for his name is the very essence of the Father's intention, but sadly the name of Jesus

> Respect for God's name was an essential part of the Ten Commandments.

is often used as a profanity on the lips of the ungodly. But the story would be different should a miraculous healing be delivered *in the name of Jesus*! Young David ran out towards the giant Goliath, shouting, "I come against you *in the name of the* LORD." As the giant fell, a healthy respect for God's name emerged (1 Sam. 17)! And similarly, when Peter stopped at the Beautiful Gate saying, "*In the name of Jesus Christ of Nazareth,* rise up and walk" it was not just the lame man giving glory to that name on that day (Acts 3:6–9 NKJV). Later, when attending court to give account for this miracle, Peter's explanation was clear—that it was "*by the name of Jesus Christ*...this man stands here before you in good health" (emphases added to the above verses). Not being one to miss an evangelistic opportunity, he then continued by proclaiming in Acts 4:10–12, "There is salvation in no one else; for there is no other name under heaven that has been given among men by which we must be saved." The essence of praying in the name of Jesus is to ask the question—What Would Jesus Pray? A modern WWJP to add to the WWJD.[5]

35

Treat others as you want to be treated

MATTHEW 7:12; LUKE 6:31

For some, this command prompts mental gymnastics, for it teaches that we should treat others as we would *like* to be treated, not as we *are* treated. For those who have endured a lifetime of mistreatment and who basically expect little else, it is an important question to ask—how would you really like to be treated? The answer then becomes the marker against which to measure your behavior towards others.

Jesus describes this as a kind of royal law, a law like love, to sum up all laws. "This is the Law and the Prophets," he says, as though this is really what Moses and the prophets were inferring, but never quite found the words. Jesus, however, hit the nail squarely on the head! Laws are about treating people justly, and as we ourselves are ultimately the best judges of how we would wish to be treated. This provides us with the perfect framework, our *royal law* for treating others.

The application of this can sometimes become a little complex. For example, a treat for me would be sitting on the sofa watching a football match, with cream cakes at half time. However, my wife would not consider any of these things to be a treat. So, my challenge is to work out what would be a treat for her. We need to apply the wisdom behind this command if a genuine blessing is to be fulfilled. For example, if our preference is for solitude, we cannot ignore others just because we would

Graham Warner

rather be left alone. Just as we appreciate our needs being met, so we must seek to meet the needs of those around us, which vary from individual to individual. In essence this principle sums up so many of Jesus's instructions like: give to those who ask, forgive those who mistreat us, treat kindly those who abuse us and our possessions, etc.

I value the use of the word *treat* in some of our Bible versions, because a treat is doing something special to make someone happy. Come on, let's spread a little happiness! I equally appreciate other versions use of "*do* unto others as you would have them *do* to you" for it implies more than just an attitude—it is an action. If we are to outwork Jesus's command in a tangible way, we must bless people with actions, not just words!

> I value the use of the word 'treat'…
> because a treat is doing something special to make someone happy.

36

Enter by the narrow gate

MATTHEW 7:13; LUKE 13:24

Enter by the narrow gate; for the gate is wide, and the way is broad that leads to destruction, and many are those who enter by it. For the gate is small and the way is narrow that leads to life and few are those who find it" (Matt. 7:13–14). This chapter of Matthew's gospel finishes with a series of twos: two gates, two ways, two kinds of fruit, two types of tree, and two houses being built—one on the rock and the other on the sand. Each option has an alternative, and indicates that deliberate choices must be made if we are to follow Jesus.

The statement, "enter by the narrow gate," is more of an invitation than a command, as in Moses's day when the Lord announced: "I have set before you life and death, the blessing and the curse. So choose life in order that you may live" (Deut. 30:19). There are two gates...and Bill Gates is not one of them! One is broad and the other narrow. A common misconception is that just one exists—the narrow gate—and that the starting point for all is the broad road. However, our passage seems to suggest that entering must be via one gate or the other, and so here the business of choosing begins. We then follow the road of our choice, broad or narrow.

The narrow gate aptly depicts the prerequisites for entry to the kingdom. The gate is narrow and small; narrow so that we can take nothing with us and small so that we need to bow low to enter. As that lovely hymn, "Rock of Ages" describes, "Nothing in my hand I bring, simply to your cross I cling".[6] We enter this gate with nothing but dependence on Christ alone. We also can enter no other way than with humility. "Except you humble yourself like a little child you can in no way enter the kingdom of God."

> There are two gates...
> and Bill Gates is not one of them!

Luke 13:24 says, "Strive to enter by the narrow door." The striving is possibly more attributable to counting the cost and dealing with hangups, rather than struggling with the gate itself. This gate, incidentally, is always open. Just like the gates of the New Jerusalem (Rev. 21:25), they shall never be shut! There is a welcome for all. Even though this way may be narrow, it is the only way to discover real life, because of the breadth of experience we gain when walking with the Lord. Jesus describes this experience as being really free (John 8:36). So, it is a freeway in every sense of the word!

37

Beware of false prophets

MATTHEW 7:15

There are two pathways: one which the Lord encourages us to take—the narrow road; and the other, the broad road leading to destruction, down which the false prophets herd those they have deceived. Jesus describes these tricksters as "ravenous wolves," whose outward garments are more identifiable with harmless sheep. False prophets and counterfeits

> We must therefore guard against underestimating the powers of false prophets.

have always existed, seeking to distract people from the truth. Back in Pharaoh's day, magicians could even mimic the signs and wonders of God (as outworked through Moses). They transformed their staffs into serpents by sorcery (I know what you're thinking—some staff don't need transforming, they already behave like serpents!), they also turned water into blood...and even created frogs! We must therefore guard against underestimating the powers of false prophets. Jesus predicted that false christs and false prophets would arise and perform great signs and wonders, with intent to mislead, were it possible, even the elect (Matt. 24:24). Fortunately, Jesus provided us with a key to enemy recognition—false prophets would be distinguishable by their fruits (Matt. 7:16–19). He applied the logic that, as thorn bushes are unable to produce grapes, or thistles figs, so bad trees are unable to produce good fruit. Amusingly, Pharoah's magicians were only able to produce the bad signs, i.e. those things by which they were already being cursed, thus making matters worse! Jesus twice repeated in Matthew chapter 7 that "you will know them by their fruits."

The two fruits in frame in this passage would seem to be doing the will of the Father in heaven, and a personal friendship with Jesus. "Not everyone who says to me, 'Lord, Lord,' will enter the kingdom of heaven; but he who does the will of my Father who is in heaven. Many will say to me on that day, 'Lord, Lord, did we not prophesy in your name, and in your name cast out demons, and in your name perform many miracles?' And then I will declare to them, 'I never knew you; depart from me, you who practice lawlessness'" (Matt. 7:21–23). A cause for concern here is that these false prophets were so utterly deceived that they had even deceived themselves into believing that they were serving Jesus. Although their power ministry included casting out demons and working miracles they were nevertheless still false prophets. So, how are we to identify their falsehood? The answer must be by examining their fruits of obedience to the rest of the words of Jesus—are they building their houses upon the rock?

38

Build your house on the rock

MATTHEW 7:24–27; LUKE 6:47

The Sermon on the Mount concludes with some brilliant picture language, with which some of us have been familiar since Sunday school days: two men, each building houses, one on the sand and the other on the rock. This is more of an observation than a command, but I shall include this parable under the guise of an implied command, for it encapsulates the very essence of this book: The wise man building on the rock is he who *hears* the sayings of Jesus and *does* them.

This story majors on the importance of building on a firm foundation. I have been known to enquire of an audience when preaching as to the nature of this firm foundation. What is the rock? The usual response is "Jesus"—and of course Jesus is the rock. But more specifically, this passage states the rock to be his *words*—"these sayings of mine." Furthermore, I believe that Jesus is not making reference here to his generalized teaching, but to this specific set of words (i.e., The Sermon on the Mount). This sermon forms the backbone of the challenge to set life on a secure footing; it is Jesus's "get it right from the start" material—the foundational Alpha Course[7] of the first century. Begin here! The ABC of discipleship.

> Here Jesus proposes radical lifestyle changes, in just about every area of life.

Anyone fashioning life upon the principles found in this sermon will find the keys to personal transformation. Here Jesus proposes radical lifestyle changes, in just about every area of life. This sermon contains

Graham Warner

the ingredients of a perfect recipe for relating to Jesus. If we love him, we will adhere to these principles, not as a test, but to please him, and to express friendship. Furthermore, living by these rules will also ensure obedience to the Father in heaven; it is the Father's will that we hear and follow his Son.

Matthew's account of this story implies that the foolish man is busy building down on the sand, while the wise man is working away on the cliff top. Is that your mental picture? Luke's account indicates that they are actually both on the sand, but the wise man digs downwards until he exposes the rock upon which to build. The foolish man considers this approach to be too much trouble, and also rather negative, given that a building ultimately should grow upwards, not downwards. He was lazy, and so he built without foundations. What is the moral of this tale? We need to spend time digging into the Word to expose these essential sayings of Jesus (i.e., the rock upon which to build)!

39

Much is required from all who have received much

LUKE 12:48

However, it could be dangerous to dig too deeply, for increased understanding means that more is required of us! On the other hand, the more we have, the more we shall have given to us! Jesus says, "To everyone who has shall more be given, but from the one who does not have, even what he does have shall be taken away" (Luke 19:26). Strictly speaking, our title is once again an observation more than a command, but as it describes criteria by which the Lord will judge us, it seems to assume the status of an implied command.

> "If you want a job done, ask a busy man."
> A busy person will often accomplish more than someone with nothing on his agenda.

The context of this principle is an illustration about slaves and their masters. Jesus explains that a faithful and sensible servant will conduct his duties in an appropriate manner and to an established schedule, even if the master delays his return. But the wicked slave parties, gets drunk, and forsakes his duties. How will the master react? Obviously, he will cut up the lazy servant into tiny pieces, chew him up, spit him out, and then subject him to a severe flogging! Well, perhaps that is a little overstated—but not by much. See Luke 12:46–48! Harsh it may be, but after all, this slave was rather naughty! I love these rather dramatic statements. Actually, I am sure this is Jesus's way of using humor to make a point, much as I have done here! Jesus continues that if we know what to do, but don't do it, we will also receive a severe flogging; but if we don't know what to do, so can't do it, we will receive but a few flogs!

The bottom line of this principle is that we should be responsible with what we have, be it duties, responsibilities, knowledge, or revelation. As with the parable of the talents, we need to use what has been entrusted to us. The servant who buried his one talent was described as wicked. The Lord expects returns on his investments. If he has invested heavily in us, he will require much in return. The guys who received five and two talents respectively were expected to use them to accrue profit, and did so. The talent buried by the wicked servant was recovered and given to the man with five talents, thus affirming this current principle.

There is a familiar phrase which states that "If you want a job done, ask a busy man." A busy person will often accomplish more than someone with nothing on his agenda. If we are faithful with our gifts and ministries, the Lord will entrust more to us! Another parable teaches that faithful servants will be given responsibility over ten or five cities, having demonstrated their faithfulness with a small agenda (Luke 19:17–19).

It seems to me that the parable of the talents is partly about initiative taking, as the recipients of the talents were given no instructions as to what to do. They did or in one case did not use their creativity to make something out of what they were given. The big question is—are we finding ways to use to the full all that the Lord has invested in us?

40

Follow me

LUKE 9:57–62; JOHN 12:26; LUKE 14:27

"Follow me" was the challenge set before several individuals as Jesus confronted them at various points in his ministry. One of the most dramatic was Matthew, who was sitting collecting taxes for the Romans. He simply stood up and left everything to follow Jesus (Matt. 9:9; Luke 5:27–28). When Matthew wrote his gospel, he related his own life-changing story in just one verse, and even then used the third person singular, as if anonymously. Had I been Matthew, I would probably have told my story at length, perhaps a chapter or two at least. How remarkably humble these disciples were!

Luke 9:57-62 charts three would-be followers of Jesus. The first says, "I will follow you wherever you go." Now that's the spirit! Wherever you lead, Lord, I will follow; whatever you do, I will do; however you are, I will be! That is the Matthew-type commitment, and surely one worth encouraging. However, the Lord replies to this man, "Foxes have holes, and the birds of the air have nests, but the Son of Man has nowhere to lay his head." His reply seems to be saying to this individual, are you really sure? Do you really understand the cost involved in your desire to follow? This man was probably intending to become a "words only" follower, i.e. one who loves to hear and to talk, but has no intention of actually *being* or *doing*.

The second would-be follower is not so keen to volunteer as the first man. Jesus challenges this man to follow, but he forestalls the commitment by saying "Let *me first* go and bury my father" (emphasis added). This *me first* approach cannot work, because Jesus requires first place. Had the father just died, the request may have been legitimate, but I fear that not to be the case. The father was probably very much alive and well, with no prospect of "pegging it" for years! "Allow the dead to bury their own dead," said Jesus. Ouch!! We are discussing family here! We can only deduce that Jesus was intending to rescue this man from a spiritually dead family, so that he could go on and proclaim the gospel to a lost world. "Go and proclaim everywhere the kingdom of God" (v 60). The spiritually dead could be left to handle burying their dead when the time came. What do you think he did?

> Jesus says, "Follow me."
> What will your excuse be?

The third would-be follower also seems to have a fair request, "Let me go and say goodbye to my family." But in essence Jesus replies, "Don't look back. No one putting his hand on the plough should ever turn back" (v 62). Jesus says, "Follow me." What will your excuse be?

41

I desire mercy and not sacrifice

MATTHEW 9:13; 12:7

If I were to put this title into my own words, I would use the phrase, "I desire social action not acts of church worship!" because amazingly this seems to be what Jesus is saying. I have often puzzled over the statement "I desire mercy and not sacrifice," and that is precisely what Jesus requires, for he says, "Go and learn what this means." So I should probably stop here and leave this page blank for your own meditation! But that would be impossible for me, because I am a teacher and teachers have to teach! Sorry, I don't do blank pages! However, you could close this book for a while and do some thinking of your own. "Go and learn what this means" is, after all, a stand-alone command in itself; but do come back!

Welcome back! One way of looking at this is to consider it less of a command to us, and more of a statement about God's own heart to exercise mercy. He is more willing to show mercy and forgiveness than he is to have us offer sacrifices to him. David said in Psalm 51:16–17, "You do not delight in sacrifice, otherwise I would give it; you are not pleased with burnt offering. The sacrifices of God are a broken spirit; a broken and a contrite heart, O God, you will not despise." David had sinned in a manner for which there were no appropriate sacrifices (i.e. adultery and murder) and that is probably the reference here. Under the Law, adultery and murder were punishable by death, so the only sacrifice he could have offered was himself! The fact that God forgave him must have been somewhat of a relief.

On the other hand, this phrase could be saying that God desires us to exercise mercy and forbearance toward fellow men, rather than offer sacrifices to God. Although it is not an outright command, it is revealing God's heart that we actively exercise mercy, thereby implying a command.

Hence the alternative phrase proposed at the start—"I desire social action, not worship!" Notice he doesn't even say, "I desire mercy *and* sacrifice." Could the Lord actually care more about how we treat the needy than he does about how we perform acts of church worship? It seems that the Lord prefers that we serve the poor instead of serving him in sacrifice. If we genuinely learn the meaning of this, there would be significant implications regarding church life. Matthew 12:7, just four chapters later, shows that Jesus's listeners had not worked out the meaning of this phrase as he had requested. I hope you did! But here he rebukes them, "If you had known what this means, 'I desire compassion not a sacrifice,' you would not have condemned the innocent.'" The Pharisees had condemned the disciples for eating ears of grain quite innocently on the Sabbath day. It is all too easy to sacrifice those around us, rather than exercising mercy towards them!

> Could the Lord actually care more about how we treat the needy than he does about how we worship him?

42

Put new wine into new wineskins
MATTHEW 9:17; MARK 2:21–22; LUKE 5:36–38

Here are some very practical DIY ideas for life! Read here for tips about wine-making and repairing torn clothing—batches and patches, I like to call it! The advice is to decant your latest batch of wine into fresh wineskins, and to use shrunken cloth to patch an old garment. Ignoring this wisdom could ruin a favourite garment and, even worse, a whole batch of wine! There is, however, a serious moral to these lessons, which come in answer to a question concerning the behavior of Jesus's disciples and those of John the Baptist. "Why do we and the Pharisees fast, but your disciples do not fast?" (Matt. 9:14). Jesus explains that wedding guests don't fast while the bridegroom is still present; it is of course a time of celebration, for eating and drinking, not fasting.

It would not be fitting to impose a Pharisaical fast at a wedding. The challenge is to work out what is appropriate behavior in any given situation. What was once appropriate may no longer be fitting. To automatically expect Jesus's disciples to do what John's had done—in this case, to fast—may not be suitable at this specific time. This gives us permission to think about why we are doing the sort of things we do. It is not necessary to do what we have always done. Just as new wine requires new wineskins, so new ideas may need new structures to contain them. Disciples need to have their wits about them, constantly questioning what is appropriate for each situation.

> The challenge is to work out what is appropriate behaviour in any given situation. What was once appropriate may no longer be fitting.

We often hear about the new wineskins scenario in connection with the work of the Holy Spirit. The Lord does new things, and we need new ways of containing this new life. I have been involved in church planting for many years, and when starting a new church, it is feasible to break from traditional practices and forms of worship. Something new can be achieved while being mindful that our *new somethings* seem to get old very quickly! We have the opportunity to experience the freedom of reinventing ourselves, limited only by our imagination—and the Bible of course! But it is infrequently that we hear about the wisdom of the old patch. If new wine requires new wineskins, then old garments require old patches. Herein lies the balance; we need to be equally aware of what is fitting for the older setting. It is foolish to force something new into something that is old—it can result in tearing and spoiling. Sadly, we too often try to put new patches in inappropriate places. Jesus teaches us to develop our diplomacy skills, to learn what fits where, for a particular moment in time. Learning these lessons will result in courage to change what needs to be changed, and skills to patch what needs to be patched.

43

Ask the Lord of the harvest to send out laborers

MATTHEW 9:38; LUKE 10:2

Life in all its richness grows abundantly throughout the world. Television programs such as *Planet Earth*[8] graphically demonstrate the fruitful nature of life, and this natural fruitfulness is mirrored by things spiritual. The harvest is not only ripe but also plentiful, says Jesus, in reference to a spiritual harvest. We do not need to pray for a harvest; harvest is not the problem. The problem is the lack of laborers to reap it. God produces the ripeness of the spiritual harvest fields, which is why he is described as the "Lord of the harvest." The book of Acts records the truth of this principle—the harvest was so abundant that we read of thousands being converted, sometimes in vast numbers, at any one time.

If we believe that the harvest is plentiful, it will motivate us to go and gather the fruit. Every church, according to Jesus, is surrounded by many who are actively or passively seeking him. Potential converts, like ripe fruit, are just waiting to be gathered. It's true our experience can often seem to be contrary to that. People seem to be disinterested in Christianity, but nonetheless, Jesus states that there are many who are desperately seeking God. Our task is to find these lost sheep. It may require much diligence on our part in seeking them out, but they are certainly there.

It is challenging to read the Old Testament laws regarding harvesting.

The poor were permitted to enter the fields and gather grapes and olives for their own consumption, but were not allowed to harvest them (Deut.

> If we believe that the harvest is plentiful, it will motivate us to go and gather the fruit.

23:24–25). Does the rather sparse gathering of converts in our current spiritual harvests perhaps make a statement about our spiritual poverty? When we are in partnership with the one who owns the fields, the Lord of the harvest, we are at liberty to harvest on a grand scale. At present, it is almost as if we are gleaning in the fields, not harvesting.

So, if we are not harvesting big time, wherein lies the problem? It is not the harvest—that is plentiful—it is the workers who are absent! That is why Jesus calls us to pray for laborers. This is a simple request to which we could all respond. Is the church in decline because of neglect in this area? When the disciples prayed about this issue, they became the answer to their own prayers, for Jesus anointed them and sent them out into the harvest fields. So be careful! Think twice before fulfilling this command, as you could find yourself in the mission field!

44

Go and bear much fruit

JOHN 15:1–8, 16

Taking some time out from a busy teaching schedule during a church house party, I took a stroll along some Danish country lanes. Dusk was just beginning to fall and I was enjoying a few moments of privacy, singing and praying out loud in the quietness of the half-light. With almost every step, I could hear the scurrying feet of wildlife (probably desperate to escape the dreadful singing) scuttling this way and that in the roadside ditches. Suddenly, my mind grasped the words of an old hymn that I was singing: "Something lives in every hue, Christless eyes have never seen."[9] This truth came home to me. How incredibly fruitful natural life is!

Throughout the world, vegetation, animal, and insect life flourishes, most of it quite spontaneously. How wonderfully has nature fulfilled the commands of its creator to reproduce and fill up the earth. As I walked along, my memory recalled similar lanes along which I would pray back at home. How many times had I watched the seedtimes turn to harvest? How often had I marvelled at the combine harvesters, reaping awesomely massive crops? They seemed to rebuke the smallness of my own fruitfulness for God. Why is it that the God of life and abundant fruitfulness is so successful in every sphere of life except the very one for which he gave his own life?

Graham Warner

Fruitfulness is God's intention for every disciple. Painfully, he prunes some of us to make us more fruitful, expressing his ultimate desire that we bear much fruit. By our fruitfulness the Father is glorified, and it is in this way that we prove ourselves to be real disciples (John 15:8). Cer-

> Jesus' parable of the sower sets a target to reproduce thirtyfold, sixtyfold, or onehundredfold. We should set this as a minimum objective for every church member.

tainly, some of this fruit refers to our qualities of character, defined as the fruits of the Spirit in Galatians 5:22. But nevertheless, the illustration of nature surely challenges us to increase our productivity, to produce fruit not just within ourselves, but also in the world around us. Jesus's parable of the sower sets a target to reproduce thirtyfold, sixtyfold, or one hundredfold. We should set this as a minimum objective for every church member, to reproduce at least thirtyfold in their lifetime. How about setting the objective to see the seed of your life bring between thirty to a hundred people to new life in Christ before your death? The church would grow phenomenally! Why not go completely over the top and make this an annual target? After all, that is what happens in nature season upon season. Jesus also adds, in John 15, that our fruit should "remain." Here is the difference between the spiritual and the natural—natural fruit decays, whereas the spiritual fruit remains forever!

45

Go, saying the kingdom of heaven is at hand

MATTHEW 10:7; LUKE 10:9–11

Here is an entire evangelism training program in one sentence! If you are looking for a presentation of the gospel that you can learn, this is it! How easy is that? All you need to say is "The kingdom of heaven is at hand." This is a positive message to deliver to the world: "Heaven is at hand." We are not instructed to threaten people with a "turn or burn," or "hell is nigh" theology. The gospel, by definition, is good news, not bad news. In essence the message is that heaven is so close that you can reach out and touch it. It is within everyone's grasp. That is the literal sense of something being at hand. As I type this, my keyboard is at hand, as is the phone, my pens, and notebook. They are all sufficiently close for me to reach out and take them with little movement. They are all within my grasp where I am, right now. Jesus is declaring that heaven is available to *all,* not just in the future, but here and now. God's healing, his love, and his joy are so close that we can reach out and take them.

Our task is to bring this heaven near to people. Paul quotes in Romans 10:6–8 and Deuteronomy 30:11–14: "It is not too difficult for you, nor is it out of reach. It is not in heaven that you should say, 'Who will go up to heaven for us to get it for us?' Nor is it beyond the sea, that you should say, 'Who will cross the sea for us to get it for us?' But the word is very near you, in your mouth and in your heart, that you may observe it." Our message echoes the words of the Lord's prayer: "Your kingdom come. Your will be done, On earth as it is in heaven" (Matt. 6:10). As you read this, heaven is very close. Jesus asks me to say this to you. If you need a touch from heaven right now, reach out and receive. It is within your grasp!

Paul described us as living in the overlap of the ages. We are those upon whom the ends of the ages have come (1 Cor. 10:11). We are living in heaven and at the same time, in the world. Soon the world will pass away, and then we shall experience heaven in all its fullness.

But the kingdom of heaven began to be released on earth two thousand years ago in Jesus. The gospel writers often mixed their terminology of "the kingdom of God" with "the kingdom of heaven" and these phrases seem interchangeable. "Heal those ... who are sick and say to them, the kingdom of God has come near to you" (Luke 10:9, 11). This is our priv-

> We are not instructed to threaten people
> with a 'turn or burn' or 'hell is nigh' theology.

ilege: to be the channels through whom God's kingdom invades the earth.

46

Heal the sick

MATTHEW 10:8; LUKE 9:2; LUKE 10:9

"Heal the sick, raise the dead, cleanse the lepers, cast out demons" (Matt. 10:8) What a command! But wait ... isn't this instruction for the twelve apostles because they were special? This was surely their commission? And if taken literally, did it not refer to the lost sheep of the house of Israel? So, surely these rather sensational orders do not apply to us today? Certainly, the Jews were to be the initial focus, but Jesus later included the rest of the world when he gave us the great commission. Mark 16:17–18 also describes signs that will accompany all believers, which includes "laying hands on the sick and they shall recover." We must bear in mind that the disciples were instructed not only to observe *everything* that Christ had commanded, but also to train their converts to obey *everything* that he taught (Matt. 28:20). So this has become an essential part of discipleship training, and that is the very purpose of this book, to look at *everything* he said and to let it train us for action. Healing was very much part of his "heaven here and now" approach to evangelism.

Thirty-five percent of Matthew's gospel describes signs and wonders such as healings and miracles. In addition to the times when Jesus healed multitudes, there are twenty-one personal testimonies of individual healings. These proved Jesus was the Messiah by the fulfilment of Old Testament Scriptures (e.g. Isa. 53:4; 32:3–4; 35:5–6; c.f Acts 2:22, etc.) That is why Jesus said, "The very works that I do, bear witness of me" (John 5:36). "Believe me...otherwise believe on account of the works themselves" (John 14:11). Certainly this was proof enough for John the Baptist, who believed without a doubt when he heard the report that the blind had received their sight and the lame walked; the lepers were being cleansed; the deaf were hearing; and the dead had been raised (Matt. 11:5). John, in his gospel, reminds us that Jesus did many more than

just these miracles: "Many other signs therefore Jesus also performed...
which are not written in this book; but these have been written that you

> Jesus healed everybody who came to him for healing. No one who asked went away with the affliction with which they came.

may believe that Jesus is the Christ, the Son of God, and that believing you may have life in his name" (John 20:30–31). These miraculous manifestations also prove something else very significant—that God cares about people, and that he desires to deal with their suffering. These miracles are clear demonstrations of God's love for mankind. Jesus healed *everybody* who came to him for healing. No one who asked went away with the affliction with which they came. He healed *every* kind of sickness and *every* kind of disease (Matt. 9:35). He now gives the church gifts of healings in order to continue this ministry (1 Cor. 12:9). Allow the Lord to use your heart and your hands to express his love for the people of the world today.

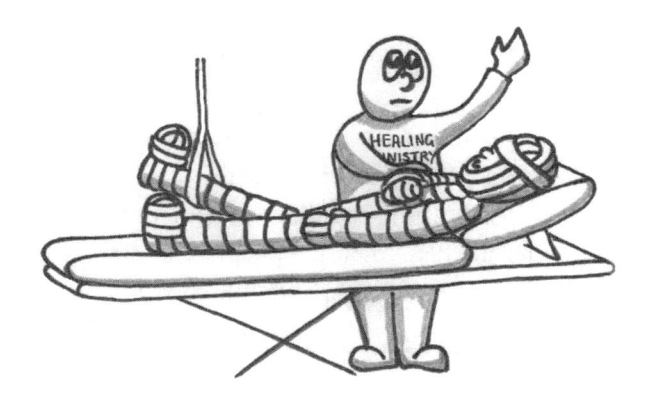

Raise the dead

MATTHEW 10:8

I recall one evangelistic occasion at Speaker's Corner in Hyde Park, London, when a professional heckler persisted in drowning me out with his top of the voice catcalling. Strangely, this attracted the curious, and the crowd swelled rapidly. But he continued to repeat the same taunting, time and again, which was, "Go on, raise the dead! If you believe in Jesus, raise the dead! Go on, raise the dead!" Eventually, I responded to the situation with the retort, "OK, I will!" Addressing the crowd, I said, "This man wants me to raise the dead, so I am going to do that right in front of you." I invited the heckler to the front, whereupon I explained that a person without Christ is described as spiritually dead in their sins. My intention, therefore, was to raise this man from spiritual death; I reached out and laid my hands on him, and suddenly, he fled with such speed that he couldn't be seen for dust!

Was Jesus referring here to raising people from their death in trespasses and sins? I don't think so. Frightening though this may seem, I

> Jesus of course demonstrated this with Lazarus, Tabitha, the centurion's servant, and the widow's son.

am convinced he was referring to physical death and physical resurrection. We may need to be selective with this one; otherwise there could be an overcrowding problem. Perhaps we should just raise the nicer people! I jest!

This command is particularly appropriate where death has been cruelly premature. No, I haven't fulfilled this one—yet! But the point is I would not rule it out. Whether I will ever do such a thing will, I'm sure, depend on the circumstances ... and my obedience! But I firmly believe that it is possible, and have heard of various instances; in fact, a person who had been raised from the dead once stayed at my home! Of course, Jesus demonstrated this with Lazarus, Tabitha, the centurion's servant, and the widow's son. Resurrection was also practised by the early church as with Eutychus, the guy whose name means "fortunate," who unfortunately fell from an upstairs window! Fortunately for him, Paul was prepared to obey Jesus in this command (Acts 20:9). Interestingly, the early church did not raise James or Steven from the dead, or anyone else who had been martyred. Martyrdom earns special rewards, and I guess they would have been pretty cross to have been robbed of these rewards because someone raised them from the dead. Mind you, they could have perhaps doubled their rewards by being martyred a second time!

48

Cast out demons

MATTHEW 10:8; MARK 16:17

We have, in our time, cast out many of these "sulphurous cackling spirits of evil," as Frank Peretti might call them! A host of demons surround us; they push, pull, and manipulate the world for evil, but largely prefer to remain hidden, working surreptitiously behind the scenes. The fruits of their labors, however, are much in evidence. It is only now and then, when the spiritual temperature is increased, that they are forced to openly manifest themselves. And so it was when Jesus was teaching with authority in the synagogue and a demonized man screamed out, "What do we have to do with you, Jesus of Nazareth? Have you come to destroy us? I know who you are – the Holy One of God" (Mark 1:24–26). Why did this demon blow its cover, when it could have remained hidden in the crowd? I envisage the demon restraining its mouth with both hands, desperately trying to hold back, but finding it impossible. A demon drawing attention to itself in front of Jesus will inevitably lose the battle. "Be quiet and come out of him," Jesus said, and with convulsions and loud cries, this unclean spirit obeyed.

> They were instructed by Jesus not to rejoice that the demons were subject to them, even though they were!

Similarly, when Jesus alighted from the boat at Gadara, having just quelled the storm with a simple "Peace, be still!" he was confronted by a different storm—this time in an individual—a demonized man known as Legion, because he hosted so many demons (a Roman legion would be apparently 3000-6000 strong—so he had a few!). You will be familiar with the narrative—where the demons came out of Legion and instead entered a herd of swine, which then cascaded down the hillside into the sea (Matt. 8:28–34). The question is why did this man run from his home amongst the tombs straight to Jesus? Why did he not run away and hide? There is something about the presence of Jesus that draws spirits out into the open. This explains why demons seem to be so prevalent in the gospels, following their somewhat lower profile in the Old Testament. The disciples went about rounding up the sick and demon possessed and bringing them to Jesus. Healing and casting out demons seemed to go hand in hand in his ministry to the multitudes. The disciples were trained to do likewise, and upon their return from one mission they were instructed by Jesus not to rejoice that the demons were subject to them, even though they were (Luke 10:17–20)! And they are subject to us too! We too should cast out unclean demons in the name of Jesus, wherever they manifest themselves or wherever the Holy Spirit gives discernment of a demon's presence.

49

Cleanse the lepers

MATTHEW 10:8

The fact that Jesus adds cleansing the lepers to this list seems to suggest that this activity is not the same as just healing the sick. A leper was considered to be not just an untouchable, needing to be quarantined, but also ceremonially unclean. Our last point concerned casting out demons; this point concerns bringing back the outcast. Although leprosy is no longer the same kind of curse that it was historically, there are modern-day equivalent diseases, such as AIDS, cancer, or dementia. Here Jesus is giving us permission to deal with contagious and incurable diseases.

Unless God healed the leper, there was no hope. No medical remedy existed, so only a priest, not a doctor, could proclaim him cleansed. Today we have parallel illnesses to which there is no known cure. We need to keep praying that medical solutions will be forthcoming via the realms of scientific research and development, but in the meantime the onus is on us to seek supernatural solutions. We need to follow the example of medical science, which relentlessly pursues scientific advance, and is ultimately committed to finding cures. Too often we give up prematurely before breaking through with supernatural healings. Our faith too easily balks at the hopeless, when it is in these very areas that Jesus commands us to freely give.

It is good news that the signs of the kingdom are that the blind see, the deaf hear, the lame walk, and that the dead are raised, because these all fall into the category of non-psychosomatic illnesses. We know that

> The more impossible it seems, the easier it should become because the Lord has to do it!

some illnesses can be induced or aggravated by negative mental processes, and in the same way I believe some healings can be achieved by positive mental processes. Mind over matter can produce a very powerful result, but that is not what we are discussing here. Were we just referring to healing headaches and backaches, there could be reason to think the healing was induced by positive thinking alone. But there is nothing psychosomatic about raising the dead! This is Jesus healing! Only God can do this! Cleansing the lepers was in the "only God can do" category, as is any other disease for which there is no known cure. Today Jesus sends us out with the same instructions as he sent out those early disciples: "As you go, preach, saying the 'kingdom of heaven is at hand,' heal the sick, raise the dead, cast out demons, cleanse the lepers" (Matt. 10:7-8). The more impossible it seems, the easier it should become, because the Lord has to do it!

50

Do not hinder those casting out demons

LUKE 9:50

The New Testament encourages us not to *quench* the Holy Spirit, which can be done in a variety of ways, not least of course is by sinning! Nor should we quench what he does through people, for example we should not despise prophesying (1 Thess. 5:19–20). Paul also instructs us not to *grieve* the Holy Spirit (Eph. 4:30). I think *grieve* is such a beautiful expression. Alternatives could have been, "Do not anger the Holy Spirit" or "Do not kindle the Spirit's fury or wrath." But grieving is such a gentle emotion, which demonstrates the exquisite forbearance and tolerance of the Lord, even though we must sometimes frustrate and anger him by our behavior and sin.

Tolerance is one attribute which cannot be ascribed to the disciples of Jesus. How they would have loved to call down fire from heaven to consume those who hindered them! (Luke 9:54). How often I would have loved to do that too! After all, there are a few choice Old Testament precedents for doing this kind of thing. One of the prophets (1 Kings 20:36) proclaimed, "Because you have not listened to the voice of the Lord, behold, as soon as you have departed from me, a lion will kill you". And sure enough this came to pass! Actually, when the disciples wanted to call down fire to consume Jesus's opponents, he reproached them with, "You don't know what kind of spirit you are of; for the Son of Man did not come to destroy men's lives, but to save them" (Luke 9:55–56). Now, that's a shame! Because it might be fun calling down fire from heaven!

The statement which provides our title here, "Do not hinder those casting out spirits in the name of Jesus," was a consequence of the disciples' encounter with a person stealing their thunder. Someone was casting out spirits, but was not part of their denomination! "We put a stop to that one!" they said to Jesus (Luke 9:49). Actually those are my w but that was the gist of the conversation! Surprisingly Jesus replied "Don't hinder them," then pronounced this little gem, "He who is not against you is for you." Satan would not cast out Satan or else his kingdom would be divided. If it were divided it would not stand. Whatever the identity of this person, he was using the name of Jesus. This of course says something about that *name*—and also about this person. Even if he wasn't part of the team, he was obviously on the same side, hence the admonishment to encourage, not hinder him.

Jesus also puts the other side to this one a couple of chapters later in Luke 11:23: "He who is not with me is against me, and he who does not

> Satan would not cast out Satan or else his kingdom would be divided. If it is divided, it would not stand.

gather with me, scatters." So, think about this: "He who is not against me is for me" and "He who is not with me is against me." Can you spot the difference?

A Real Apprentice   115

Freely you have received, freely give

MATTHEW 10:8

To make neither charge nor profit is the spirit of Jesus. He gave, asking for nothing in return. When he challenges people to give up their worldly possessions, the object was never to fund his own ministry or that of his evangelistic team. Rather, his agenda was to encourage people to give so that *the poor may receive*. I personally grow a little tired of the endless appeals for finance on Sky Television's God Channels; I also think some churches could learn an important lesson here! Jesus clearly says that whatever we have received has been free of charge, so we should likewise give freely to others.

> They would never lack and would never be able to out-give God!

We could interpret this statement slightly differently— Jesus could be saying that because we have abundantly received the blessings of the kingdom, such as manifold healings, freedom from death or demons, all given so generously by the Father, that we should be equally liberal and generous in releasing these blessings to others. Yes, I am sure this is also correct! And what a challenge! How generous are we when it comes to raising the dead and casting out demons? Freely you have received, freely give. Jesus is surely expecting that we engage in these activities as often as possible! How free have we been in curing the incurables? I challenge myself!

He makes the point that we should also freely serve people with our finances, insisting that we should not acquire money, gold, silver, or copper. The contrasting thoughts in Matthew chapter 10 are somewhat noteworthy: Jesus has just proposed that we give freely, not acquiring gold or silver. Then he continues with the instruction to "Go—but take nothing with you, not even a bag for your journey" (Matt. 10:10, my paraphrase). One might have expected him to say, "You are going to give freely, so take as much with you as you can, so that you can be self-supporting and not be burdensome upon those you visit. Therefore take gold and silver so that you can give to people generously everywhere you go." Instead they went out to give freely, but on a physical level had nothing to give, and were totally dependent on others for their daily needs. In reality they were to exercise faith and trust that their heavenly Father would provide for their every need, as they went out to seek first the kingdom of God. The point is that actually they would always have something to give, because God would always give freely to them. They would never lack, and would never be able to out-give God!

52

Do not go from house to house

MARK 6:10; LUKE 10:7

If you are earnestly seeking a verse to excuse yourself from door-to-door evangelism, here it is! Unfortunately, though, this is not applicable to doorbell witnessing—sorry! The early church still witnessed from house to house. For example, Paul visited every home while in Ephesus, in order to warn everybody with his message (Acts 20:20-31). The context of this statement isn't actually evangelism. Jesus is instructing the apostles where they should/should not seek overnight hospitality.

> Jesus is instructing the apostles where they should and should not seek overnight hospitality.

He told them to find a reputable home, inquire who was worthy in the town, and then stay there until the time came to depart from that city. They were not to try to better themselves, should a more comfortable home become available the next week, but to remain loyal to the first person offering them hospitality. After all, it would be rude to move on! Also, it would have been advantageous to stay in one place in order to maximize their availability to people, for it meant that they could be readily found.

On one occasion I was speaking at some mission meetings in a northern English city. After concluding my first night's message, but before being introduced to my host (who had been due to give me hospitality for the week), a Seikh, fully regaled in turban, who had just listened to me preach, came forward and shook my hand warmly. He said, "As long as you are in this town you must stay at my house." Not wishing to miss an interesting evangelistic opportunity, I accepted his offer, asking the church to rearrange their plans. We retired to bed that night after a monumentally hot curry, through which I struggled in obedience to the command, "Eat whatever is put before you" (I am not a fan of hot and spicy foods!) As the smell of curried breakfast wafted up the stairs next morning, I desperately regretted my decision, wishing that Jesus had actually said to stay only one night in each house! By the end of the week, my tastes buds were burnt to a frazzle! But at least he had made Jesus his chief guru! Learning to accept hospitality is a grace that some of us need to acquire! But it nevertheless wins for our host a wonderful reaping of rewards, because God rewards the giver for their every kindness, even if their offering is just a cup of cold water! Particularly welcome with hot and spicy foods!

53

As you enter a house give it your greeting of peace

MATTHEW 10:13; LUKE 10:4

Perhaps this statement, as with our last point, refers only to the homes where we stay, although I prefer to believe that its application is for every home we enter. It is an interesting instruction, in that it demonstrates that we should bless places, not just people. Let your peace come on the home. We understand that places can be atmospheric—some a little eerie, and others serene and pleasant. Here Jesus seems to say that we are able to modify this atmosphere. It follows his comment about heaven being at hand; we can introduce a little heaven into people's homes with a genuine blessing of peace.

If we can do this for others, then it is logical that we also apply it to our own homes. We need Jesus to fill our homes with his presence, peace, and light. It has always puzzled me how strangers can enter our home and say, "Isn't it peaceful here!" I am puzzled because I am a panic-driven person, and always think our home is full of panic! But they seem to sense something totally different—it's Jesus, not us! If our blessing has the potential to change people's living environments, then we should maximize our opportunities to enter into people's homes. In Luke's gospel we see that Jesus had no qualms about inviting himself to the house of Zacchaeus (Luke 19:5). How about that as an evangelistic strategy? As you pass a complete stranger in the street, just say, "Let's go back to your place for a meal!" I guess that is similar to the idea we have just considered, where Jesus encouraged the disciples to find a worthy person's house and stay there until they left that particular town. Zacchaeus would not have been described as particularly worthy—quite the opposite in fact—but as a result of Jesus's visit, salvation and peace came to his house and the poor received a big blessing. You may remember he gave half of his possessions to the poor, and the victims of his extortion were recompensed fourfold.

> We can introduce a little heaven into people's homes with a genuine blessing of peace.

Note the interesting twist in the tail of this command: If a house rejects you then you should let your blessing return to you. In other words, a blessing is so tangible it must go somewhere. An illustration might be if I were to give a family a thousand pounds, and they refuse to receive it, the money would still exist. Therefore I may as well reclaim it. Rejected blessings still exist, so let them be returned to sender. What a valid reason for blessing as many people as possible, for a percentage will refuse it, resulting in many blessings bouncing back! When we are rejected, we actually become blessed—by our own blessing.

54

Even a cup of cold water

MATTHEW 10:42

"Whoever in the name of a disciple gives to one of these little ones even a cup of cold water to drink, truly I say to you, he shall not lose his reward." What a lovely way to conclude this particular sermon in Matthew 10. Having told us we should raise the dead and cast out demons, he finishes with a "by the way, don't forget to make people cups of tea!" This illustrates the perfectly balanced nature of his teaching, so that we do not become so immersed in all the big, supernatural, powerful stuff of the ministry that we forget to serve people with cups of cold water. In fact, Jesus mentions rewarding the gift of a simple drink, but says nothing about rewarding such deeds as raising the dead or healing the incurably sick. I guess those actions probably have their own rewards…I know how amazing I shall feel on the day I raise the dead!

In this passage it is difficult to ascertain whether the cup of cold water is being given or received by a Christian. Either way round, this illustration is exciting. Perhaps it is deliberately ambiguous in order to cater for both options. If Jesus is saying that any kindly act towards a Christian is valued so highly by God that he rewards the benefactor, it underlines the benefits of sending his disciples out without money and supplies; anybody serving them along their way would have been wonderfully blessed by God. "Truly they would not go without their reward."

If, however, the gift of this cup of cold water is being offered by a Christian to a non-Christian, the insight we glean from Jesus is equally exciting. The Lord watches the tiniest detail of any social action, and will reward us for every caring deed we undertake for others. Such acts are soon forgotten by us, but not by the Lord. He remembers each seemingly insignificant element of service. Not only does he remember it, but will reward each one.

Also in this context of rewards, Jesus comments in the previous verses that anyone receiving a prophet will receive a prophet's reward and anyone receiving a righteous man shall receive a righteous man's reward. How amazing are those statements? It illustrates how much God appreciates his children being received positively by the world. "He who receives you receives me, and he who receives me receives him who sent me" (v 40). In other words, should I share some prophetic message with someone, and they listen, they would be rewarded. And if people were to look at my life and conclude, "He is a righteous person" (unlikely, but if they did...!), we would both receive the same reward! Go on—I am fishing for a compliment—because we both stand to gain!

> Having told us we should raise the dead and cast out demons, he finishes with a 'By the way, don't forget
> to make people cups of tea!'

55

Shake the dust off your feet

MATTHEW 10:14; MARK 6:11; LUKE 9:5

This sentence, "shake the dust off your feet'," occurs three times in the gospels, but to my knowledge it is not something commonly practised. I do it regularly because I often work in a dusty atmosphere, but the context here is in response to rejection. The instruction occurs almost as many times as that for Communion. Perhaps like Communion services we should also have "Shaking off the dust" services! Or is it just me? Perhaps I feel rejection more than others!

Shaking off the dust possibly has most relevance as an illustration in a hot country—after all, the disciples lived in a sandy, dusty environment. Had Jesus gone to Scandinavia he would probably have used "shake off the snow," or here in England, "wipe the mud off your feet," but whatever the expression, the act is a prophetic one that addresses the problem of rejection. Rejection never feels comfortable, and it often damages the inner self. But don't become negative! Shake off the dust! Say to yourself, "I

> Shake off the dust! Say to yourself, "I will not be contaminated by this rejection."

---

will not be contaminated by this rejection." A deliberate shaking of heart and mind is needed to escape the contamination that accompanies any

124   Graham Warner

rebuff. Some readers may be needing to shake off the dust of relationships that have broken down, where the emotional pain still hurts; perhaps some have been rejected by friends and all bridges destroyed ... Well, it is time to shake the dust off your feet!

In one way this allows us to shrug off our hurting, but it also opens up the door for the Lord to respond to those who have inflicted our pain, for effectively we are "shaking off the dust *against* them." Luke 9:5 (emphasis added) says, "Shake the dust off the soles of your feet for a testimony *against* them." So this action is not just impacting the way that I deal with my inner feelings of rejection; it is also provoking a reaction from the Lord. "Truly I say to you, it will be more tolerable for Sodom and Gomorrah in the day of judgment than for that city." The thought of judgment is unpleasant; if it helps, the comment seems to relate here to cities, not houses. Matthew 10:14 mentions individual houses, "As you go out of that house or city shake off the dust," but only the *city* is mentioned in the context of judgment in verse 15: "It will be more tolerable for Sodom and Gomorrah in the day of judgment than for that *city*" (emphasis added).

This mention of judgment is the opposite of the rewards we considered in the last point. The Lord is so pleased by those who accept us that he rewards them accordingly. But he is equally devastated by those rejecting us. Again, he holds us in such high esteem that our rejection becomes as serious as the sins of Sodom and Gomorrah. Hmmm, that's amazing! Luke 10:11 adds that we should say one further thing, "Even the dust of your city which clings to our feet, we wipe off against you; yet be sure of this, *the kingdom of God has come near to you*" (emphasis added). You see how the rejection is actually not of you, but of the kingdom of God in you!

56

Be as wise as serpents and as harmless as doves

MATTHEW 10:16

It seems that God uses us as the fulcrum between judgment and rewards and I think we need to understand just how key is our role in God's process of evaluating the non-Christian world. He constantly watches us to discover how people relate to us. Is their attitude positive and accepting or negative and rejecting? Whichever it is, the Lord has taken notice. For that reason we need to be extremely careful. How frightful would it be if someone received judgment for rejecting us purely because we had been offensive or lacked wisdom in our actions? So Jesus says, "Be as wise as serpents and as harmless as doves."

I trust that you don't mind Jesus likening us to birds, animals, and reptiles. I know we sometimes shudder when Jesus referred to a Samaritan woman as a dog. She replies, "Even the dogs eat the crumbs which fall from their master's table" (Matt. 15:27). Actually, the word *dog* translates more closely as a household pet, like a "puppy," which is rather cute! What is not so cute is that Jesus refers to us as sheep! They might be cuddly but they are pretty stupid creatures. Wolves enjoy them as a tasty meal, so beware! Jesus even called Herod a sly fox, and foxes might

> He constantly watches us to discover how people relate to us.
> Is their attitude positive and accepting, or
> negative and rejecting?
> Whichever it is, the Lord has taken notice.

eat sheep for breakfast, so extreme care is advised. However, here in this passage he likens us to snakes and doves!

I wouldn't have viewed the serpent as the wisest of creatures. The owl would seem a more obvious choice. I know little about snakes (or owls for that matter!), but I think the point here is a simple one—snakes do not proactively seek trouble, at least with regard to humans. They only attack as a last resort, and prefer to avoid confrontation; therein lies their wisdom! On seven occasions Jesus slipped away through the crowds to avoid trouble. Sometimes he told people to keep secret the miracles that he had performed for them in order to avoid a clash, and there were times when he stayed out of the cities for similar reasons. Don't go looking for persecution! Hmm, I can take that advice!

Be as harmless as doves! I know little about doves either, but they seem to be passive, gentle, non-confrontational creatures. The dove is recognized as a symbol for the Holy Spirit, when he comes to rest on Jesus following baptism. We, like the dove, need to become the symbols of peace!

57

When they persecute you in this city flee to the next

MATTHEW 10:23

The apostle Paul usually moved on when ejected from his current situation, so I am sure he found comfort in these words! Persecution began the first major push into world evangelization after the early church was driven out of Jerusalem. The new Christians lost their homes, their jobs, and their non-Christian friends. If ever there were a time to feel discouraged, to put faith onto a back burner, it was then. But instead they were scattered everywhere, and everywhere they went, they shared the good news about Jesus.

> Persecution began the first major push into world evangelization, after the early church was driven out of Jerusalem.

As Christians, we live behind enemy lines, and there will be times when our position becomes untenable. Just as Jesus was rejected, so we will be rejected and repelled—we should not be surprised or discouraged by it. Incidentally, rejection should only come from the world, not the church. Sometimes we feel persecuted by church members, and feel the urge to move on to a new church as a consequence. This reminds me of a joke! May I tell jokes in a serious book about discipleship? There was a castaway stranded on a deserted island; it was many years before a ship finally passed by to rescue him. He had been good with his hands and loved DIY, so

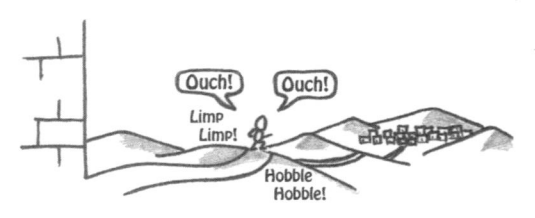

128   Graham Warner

he confidently escorted his rescuers round the island. There were two enormous buildings, and his rescuers pointed to one of them and asked, "What is this building?" He replied, "That's my church. I built it as a place to worship God." Turning and pointing towards the other building they said, "And what is that building?" He answered, "Oh, that's the church I used to go to!" Some of us would also find a reason to move on, even if we were the only person in the church!

There is perhaps a serious side to the potential persecution from within the church. Jesus was persecuted by the Pharisees, the religious people in power at the time, and the early church was persecuted by the Sadducees. Both were religious groups. Almost all of the apostle Paul's persecutors were Jews, who hounded him from city to city. Historically, it has been when church and state have jumped into bed together that some of the grossest exterminations have ensued. This world is not our home. We are seeking a heavenly kingdom. So don't be discouraged! Irrespective of whether you do or do not feel completely at home, wherever you go in this world, share the heavenly message about Jesus.

Come aside and rest a while

MARK 6:31

We all need to rest from time to time. I am glad the Old Testament had a lot of *holy days*. God seems to be very positive about taking time off! "Holiday" is a derivative of "holy day". I love holidays, although they usually come as quite a shock to my system, as I am somewhat of a semi-workaholic. Biblically, the point of holidays was taking days out to become *holy*. I think for many, holidays nowadays have become un-holy! Personally, I like the concept in the Old Testament of annual holidays; that's not taking time off *within* the year, but taking the whole year as a holiday! Seriously, every seventh year was considered to be a year off, and seven times the seventh year led to the year of Jubilee, when another year out was taken.[10] So...a two-year holiday! Imagine the suntan after a twenty-four-month holiday!

The concept of the *Sabbath* was also a sort of holiday. People were encouraged to lay aside one day in seven as a complete rest. Unfortunately, Sundays can become quite busy days. What with church and hospitality, and catching up on the week's shopping...Pardon?! Shopping on the Sabbath?! All right! I only raised this to shock! You would not find me in a shop on the Sabbath...Sunday, yes, but never on a Saturday!! Forgive my flippancy, but I think Jesus tried to make the point that Sabbath was supposed to serve us, not the other way round (Sabbath is the only one of the Ten Commandments not repeated as a command in the New Testament). I think it is the concept of rest that is the important factor, not the specific day! In fact, it is not even *rest* that is the issue—

> Our rest is not 'resting' but recharging our spiritual batteries, by plugging into the Lord and being filled afresh with the Holy Spirit.

130   Graham Warner

the point of Sabbath was to spend time with the Lord. The Law said that the Sabbath was *for* the Lord, so it is not for us to sit back and put our feet up. Actually, if I take a day off to put my feet up, I often feel more tired as a result. Real Sabbath is finding eternal, supernatural rest. Our rest is not *resting* but recharging our spiritual batteries, by plugging into the Lord and being filled afresh with the Holy Spirit. Although God took the seventh day off after creation, he actually never stopped; he neither slumbers nor sleeps. Just as well, as everything would fall apart if he took a holiday!

God doesn't have to eat to gain energy; he doesn't have to sleep to recharge his batteries; he is not dependent upon anything for his energy. He *is* eternal energy, he is perpetual motion. We were built to run on the Lord as our fuel; only then can we run and not be weary, and rise on wings as eagles (Isa. 40:31). I don't know when you find your Sabbath rest, but it is essential that you do, at least once a week. Probably not a bad idea to have some food, sleep, and a bit of physical rest too!

59

Either make the tree good and its fruit good, or make it bad

MATTHEW 12:33

"Don't be lukewarm" is the theme of the message here. Jesus proffers some strong opinions about this in the book of Revelation. Lukewarm Christians literally make him sick: "I will spew you out of my mouth" (Rev. 3:16). He would wish us to be hot, or even cold, but never somewhere in the middle. We must come down on one side or the other, not sit on the fence.

Make a decision as to which way you want to go! Do you want to be good or bad? There is a saying Roger Forster, a former colleague, often uses that: "We can sometimes have just enough of the kingdom to spoil the world, and just enough of the world to spoil the kingdom."[11] We can be guilty of trying to live with one foot in the world and the other foot in the church. I remember a young convert coming to see me in South East London, admitting that she was still trying to be a prostitute as well as a disciple of Jesus. I suggested that she should forget about discipleship and go back to being a full-time prostitute. This was tough advice, and I felt uneasy about it afterwards, because she did just that for a little while. But it wasn't long before she was back in church with a wholehearted determination to follow Jesus.

"Either make the tree good and its fruit good, or make the tree bad and its fruit bad," said Jesus. He then continued by referring to the Pharisees, whom he was addressing at the time, as a brood of vipers! No, not "wise serpents"; here he meant "bad fruit" serpents! Then he asked them (v 34), "Can you, being evil, speak what is good?" This is a clever question, to which there is no easy answer. To say no would be to admit that they could not speak what is good, and to say yes would be tantamount to admitting that they were evil! I wish I could devise clever questions like that!

> Lukewarm Christians literally make him sick—
> "I will spew you out of my mouth."

Jesus then explained that, "The good man out of his good treasure brings forth what is good; and the evil man out of his evil treasure brings forth what is evil" (v 35). He then concluded that a man can be judged by the words that he speaks, "For by your words you shall be justified, and by your words you shall be condemned" (v 37). Verse 36 states that we shall give account for every careless, useless word…oops, I may have to edit this book quite severely! Seriously, our words portray what is in our hearts.

60

Behold, behold, behold, and behold!

MATTHEW 12:41, 42, 49–50; 13:3–8

There are a few of these "beholds" throughout the gospels, (i.e. observe, see, or perceive) which alert us to pay closer attention to the particular topic of conversation. There are four *beholds* in focus in Matthew chapters 12 and 13 that result from the Pharisees asking to see a sign. They wanted to witness some magic: "Come on, do a miracle right in front of our eyes and we might believe in you." Jesus calmly suggested a few things for them to consider, and left them to meditate. He refused to give them the sort of sign they were seeking (because, as he points out, it is an evil generation that seeks for signs), but he used the opportunity however to present them with some riddles to solve. I have italicized the "beholds" in the following verses.

"As Jonah was three days and three nights in the belly of the great sea monster, so shall the Son of Man be three days and three nights in the heart of the earth. The men of Nineveh shall stand up with this generation at the judgment, and shall condemn it because they repented at the preaching of Jonah; and *behold* something greater than Jonah is here" (Matt. 12:40–41). This is easy for us to understand looking back at Jesus's three-day burial, but considerably harder for them to grasp at that time!

The second riddle is a little more immediate and simpler to understand than the first. "The Queen of the South shall rise up with this generation at the judgment and shall condemn it, because she came from the ends of the earth to hear the wisdom of Solomon; and *behold* something greater than Solomon is here" (v 42).

The third *behold* does not focus on Jesus, but on the audience listening to him. He was told that his mother and brothers were outside and wished to converse with him, to which he replied, "Who is my mother and who are my brothers?" Stretching out his hand and pointing to those in the room around him he said, "*Behold*, my mother and my brothers! For whoever does the will of my Father who is in heaven, he is my brother, and sister, and mother" (v 49–50).

From there he moved on to relate some parables about the kingdom—actually seven of them in chapter thirteen alone. But he announces the first with, "*Behold* the parable of the sower" (13:3). Each of these "beholds" present a cameo upon which to meditate. Perhaps it is worth taking a little time to consider each of these as a meditation exercise before moving on.

> He refused to give them the sort of sign they were seeking (because it is an evil generation that seeks for signs).

61

Hear then the parable of the sower

MATTHEW 13:18

Well, if you have performed the suggested meditation exercise, you will already have worked through this next point. If not, you are very naughty...so...do it now! We noted a little earlier that a good tree produces good fruit, and good fruit in the heart will determine the words that come out of the mouth. Now we look at how a good heart produces good fruit.

This must be one of the best known parables of Jesus, so I will comment only briefly. Jesus thrice emphasizes its importance by beginning, "Behold the parable" (Matt. 13:3); "He who has ears, let him hear" (v 9); and "Hear then the parable of the sower" (v 18). The parable defines those factors which prevent the seed (i.e. the Word) from being effective in our lives. Jesus presents three scenarios: the Word is **S**tolen; the Word is **S**tarved, or the Word is **S**tifled. You will be familiar with the various conditions into which the scattered seeds landed. Firstly, the Devil seeks to steal the Word from us. Sometimes I struggle to recall what the Lord has spoken to me earlier in the day ... yet at the time it was so alive and relevant. How many times have I been challenged in meetings, believing it will be life-changing, and almost instantly, the thought has evaporated? Don't let Satan snatch these precious seeds! Dig them in a little deeper, for birds will take them if they remain on the surface! We need to resow everything the Devil steals as many times as is necessary to take root.

The starved seeds falling on rocky soil grow quickly—but wither in the heat (the pressures and persecutions!) "Lord, take away my stony heart, break up the hardness in my spirit, and turn my rocky barren places into soft, fertile soil."

The stifled seeds, although developing nicely, become choked by other things growing alongside the Word. Too many anxieties and cares

> Good soil produces fruit, some a hundredfold, some sixty, and some thirty.

about life, the desire for riches and material wealth—all serve to stifle growth and the fruitfulness of what God wants to do in us.

Good soil produces fruit, some a hundredfold, some sixty, and some thirty. This is great returns for every seed sown! Imagine that every seed developing in me could bless, feed, or otherwise impact up to a hundred other people! The secret of fruitfulness is sowing the Word—not only in ourselves, but in others too!

62

Honor your father and mother

MATTHEW 15:4–7; MARK 7:10

Yes, this is a good principle—but have you seen my parents?! Surely, this one has to be conditional on the state of one's parents. I am only joking! My parents are truly honorable, and so to honor them is easy, and I have done so from my heart all my life. It is perhaps just as well, for the Old Testament Law states that anyone disobeying their parents should be put to death (Deut. 21:18–21)! Could this be the solution for the rampant disrespect of authority in the world today? Selah! (Stop for a while and meditate). Sadly, my mother has gone to be with the Lord during the process of my writing this book. However, I greatly honor every memory of her!

Demonstrating disrespect to parents would have curtailed a man's life quite considerably, as it was punishable by stoning to death. Conversely, parental respectfulness would have prolonged life, for this is the first command linked with a promise: "Honor your father and mother, as the Lord has commanded you, that your days may be prolonged, and that it may go well with you on the land which the Lord your God gives you" (Deut. 5:16).

So what does honoring parents entail? Is it a just a matter of speaking well of them? Or is it holding respect for them deep in your heart? Or is it obeying them—even when you disagree? Maybe it involves elements of all of these, but the context in which Jesus raises the issue is the physical care of parents. He is rebuking the Pharisees for transgressing the commands of God by their own traditions. They had managed to create a loophole in the duty of financial care for parents by donating funds to the synagogue instead. Clever one! I wonder who stood to gain by that little rule?!

Once again Jesus shows that God is more concerned about using money to serve people, in this case ailing or aging parents, than giving it as a form of worship to God. I really hope my children are taking note! Seriously, though, parenting is not easy and we all make mistakes. I sometimes think I would make a far better parent if I could start over again at this point in my life! And possibly your parents would say the same. I am certainly grateful for all that my parents have done for me through the years—the love, the time, the concern, the help, the wisdom, the model, the money, the spiritual training, the sacrifices...yes, and even the discipline!

> The Old Testament Law states that anyone disobeying their parents should be put to death!

63

Honor the Lord with the heart, not just lip service

MATTHEW 15:8; MARK 7:6 (IMPLIED)

These people honor me with their lips, but their hearts are far from me. They worship me in vain; their teachings are but rules taught by men" (Matt. 15:8–9 NIV). This is an observation by Jesus about hypocrites, and he applies some verses from Isaiah 29 to them. Jesus has already pointed out that it is out of the abundance of the heart that the mouth speaks, and that the fruit of the lips prove what is in the heart. So then, how does this command fit, because it seems to be suggesting the opposite? Although these hearts are cold and empty, the mouths are speaking words of praise. These words are nothing but lip service and flattery, patronizing God with lies! They have to be aware that God knows that this is all a façade. If God is not fooled, what is the point? I think the point is that everybody else is listening. This is done for no other reason than to impress their fellow men.

> Some use the same tongue to bless God as to curse men; the same mouth can pour out both blessing and cursing.

It is so easy to do. It is quite feasible to go to church, say all the right things, sing along with all the songs of praise, and yet know that your heart is not in it. An old adage says, "There are more lies sung in church on Sunday than spoken by the rest of the world for the rest of the week." True worshippers worship in spirit and truth, and truth is where the heart and mouth are in harmony. James, in his epistle 3:9-10, adds to the argument by emphasizing that some use the same tongue to bless God as to curse men, who are made in the image of God. The same mouth can pour out both blessing and cursing. He refers to the tongue as unruly, evil, untameable, and full of deadly poison (v 8). Despite the fact that it is but a tiny part of the human body, it can trigger major problems. The tongue may be likened to a small flame which is capable of setting a whole forest ablaze, or the small rudder of a great ship with the capacity to turn the whole vessel. He observes that man can tame animals, birds, reptiles, and even fish, but asks, "Who can tame the human tongue?" (vv 5–8).

Perhaps speaking in tongues may be one of the keys to this area, where the Holy Spirit gives us gifts of new tongues (languages that we have not studied), and is thereby able to use our tongues to praise, to prophesy, to proclaim, and to pray. Not only can he tame the tongue, but he can use it for purposes of glory. Jesus adds that speaking in tongues is one of the signs that would accompany those that believe (Mark 16:17). He will of course want to fill our hearts too!

64

Watch and beware of the leaven of the Pharisees
MATTHEW 16:6; MARK 8:15; LUKE 12:1

The disciples were a little confused by this statement, and presumed it referred to bread. They were probably asking each other whether the Pharisees had recently opened a dodgy bakery! Or was it because they had forgotten to eat any bread? Had they been so busy feeding the other four thousand people that they had forgotten to have any themselves? Jesus puts their minds at rest, explaining clearly that the leaven to which he was referring equated to the teaching of the Pharisees and Sadducees (Matt. 16:12). Inaccurate teaching acts like leaven, which then permeates through the whole lump, thereby corrupting it!

So, this warning is about religious leaders who preach false doctrine. He reserved some choice expressions for those who led people astray. The following are just a few examples: He described the Pharisees as "blind" five times in Matthew 23. "…blind guides of the blind. And if a blind man guides a blind man, both will fall into a pit" (Matt. 15:14). "You travel about on land and sea to make one convert; and when he becomes one you make him twice as much a child of hell as yourselves" (v 15); "You blind guides, who choke on a gnat and swallow a camel!" (v 24); "You clean the outside of the cup and of the dish, but inside they are full of robbery and self-indulgence" (v 25). "For you are like whitewashed tombs which on the outside appear beautiful, but inside they are full of dead men's bones and all uncleanness" (v 27). I have a horrible feeling that these comments are probably very similar to those heard around a Sunday lunch table when assessing my preaching in church that morning?!

Inappropriate teaching can be like poison, so we need to be mindful of what we hear. So how do we discern what is right and what is wrong teaching? Well, Jesus himself is the measure—the yardstick—by which

> "You blind guides of the blind, and if a blind man leads a blind man, both will fall into a pit."

we test all things. He is the way and the truth. Jesus provides sufficient material in the gospels to enable us to understand his heart, his lifestyle, his thinking, and his teaching. By this we judge what we hear. If my wife were accused of making a certain comment, I would instantly know whether or not she had, because I know her well enough to identify the kind of things she might say. The same principle applies to Christian teaching. The question we should therefore ask is, "Would Jesus have said this?" Given paragraph two above, his comments can be quite surprising, so be open!

65

Whatever you bind on earth will be bound in heaven

MATTHEW 16:19; MATTHEW 18:18

Keys are a frustrating fact of life. I need to carry seven of them around with me just to be able to access my home, my car, and my office. I despise keys, but appreciate just how necessary they are to keep others out of: my home, my car, and my work place! For the purposes of illustration for street preaching, I once made a huge set of keys, almost a meter long. On one occasion I recall holding one above my head, explaining this to be a replica of my car key. A youth listening in the audience retorted, "You must have a blooming big car!" I laughed my way through to the end of my street sermon, the subject of which was finding the right key to unlock life.

Keys come hand in hand with responsibility—and a sense of power. Unlocking my workshop in the morning declares it to be officially open, and locking it up in the evening, often quite late, signifies closure. This kind of power falls into a similar category as that referred to here—binding and loosing. The context in Matthew 16:19 states that we have been given the keys of the kingdom. It adds that the gates of hell will not prevail against us. So does this mean we have a key to unlock the gates of hell? How amazing would it feel if we held sufficient power to lock and unlock the Devil's gates, and could declare the official opening hours of hell? I don't think we can, for if it were so, the place would never be open for business. But we certainly can control the impact of hell on individual lives by opening doors for those who are bound, in order to set them free, and closing doors of specific demonic activity. Of course we have no human powers to do such things; we simply deploy the key, and the Lord does the rest from heaven. What we bind on earth shall be bound in heaven and what we loose on earth shall be loosed in heaven. The keys that we have been given, if not the keys to the gates

> We do possess the power to open the gates of heaven
> and, crazy as it may sound, we can declare
> the opening hours of heaven.

of hell, are certainly the keys to the kingdom of heaven. We do possess the power to open the gates of heaven and, crazy as it may sound, we can declare the opening hours of heaven. These keys are in the plural, just like the bunch of keys that weigh down my pocket. Different keys open different doors, and similarly, we hold differing keys for the various situations that confront us. We just need to find the appropriate keys. These verses prove that the Lord expects us to take the initiative; whatever key we turn is also turned in heaven.

66

Become as a child

MATTHEW 18:3; MARK 10:15 (IMPLIED)

Unless you are converted and become like children, you shall not enter the kingdom of heaven." Jesus continues "Whoever then humbles himself as this child, he is the greatest in the kingdom of heaven." Here is an amazing kingdom factoid—when a convert starts in the kingdom of God, he starts as the greatest! The only way to maintain this awesome position is to remain as humble as a child. Jesus asks that we enter his world in the same way that he entered ours. He came as a helpless baby, having emptied himself of all that he was. For us there is no other way than to be born again in a similar way, also laying aside all that we have been. To become a child of God demands a total restart. Because it takes such humility to enter God's kingdom, there are few mighty, noble, or worldly wise people who are prepared to take the plunge to these kinds of depths. But notice the

> We humble ourselves, as far as the world is concerned, lower than ever! In this moment we are simultaneously the greatest in the kingdom of heaven.

incredible contrast—we humble ourselves, as far as the world is concerned, lower than ever! In this moment we are simultaneously the great-

146   Graham Warner

est in the kingdom of heaven. These two extremes touch each other in the moment of spiritual rebirth!

Because Jesus demands that we become *like* children, it logically follows that he would welcome those who *are* children. Hence Mark 10:14 says, "Permit the children to come to me; do not hinder them; for the kingdom of God belongs to such as these." I recently received a private rebuking for comments made whilst preaching on this subject. "If you need a miracle," I suggested, "how about finding a child with faith, and ask him to pray for you. God uses such as these." Oh...I know, this may be quite diplomatically incorrect! However, I can't help but believe it to be true. I was once wonderfully healed through the simple prayer of my small daughter (seven years old at that time), when the prayers of some of the most spiritual men in the land had not broken through. Alright, I realize that all this prayer power was cumulative, but God nevertheless used a little girl, and very powerfully. On another occasion, I desperately needed to access some notes from my computer for an imminent meeting, but the wretched machine had entered some kind of terminal arrest! When my daughter realized that I was also about to have a terminal arrest she simply said, "Why don't you ask Jesus to make it work?" To which I replied, "Good idea. Why don't *you?*" The computer immediately pinged into life the moment she prayed! That's God! Actually, she was interrupting the elders meeting to say good night. Unknown to her, the elders had all been laying hands on the machine! There is no doubt something quite special about childlike faith!

67

Whoever receives one such child receives me

MATTHEW 18:5; MARK 9:37; LUKE 9:48

In my previous book, *The Evangelism Handbook*, there is an entire chapter devoted to the way God uses and reads everyday situations to ascertain people's receptiveness to his kingdom. For example, he tells us that if a non-Christian is accepting of a Christian, it is tantamount to accepting Christ in Matthew 10:40–41: "If they accept you they accept me." Likewise if he rejects a Christian, he also rejects Christ. Further, God equates serving the poor with serving Christ himself, as in Matthew 25:40ff. We shall look at these verses again a little later. But here Jesus is offering us yet another illustration—that receiving a child (or a humble convert that is like a child) is the same as receiving Christ.

I have read recently about a concept called "thin slicing."[12] This means that a complete picture can be discovered by examining just one small section, or thin slice. For example, it can be possible to establish the strength of a marriage by listening to one short conversation between a husband and wife. The likelihood of that marriage lasting can be predicted with a fairly high degree of accuracy by observing how the partners relate together in just a few moments. I wonder whether the principle of receiving this child, or the childlike, is one way that Jesus thin slices. He learns how sensitive we are to spiritual things by watching our level of responsiveness to these vulnerable people!

His actual words were, "Receive one such child *in his name*," so this is presumably referring to a disciple receiving a child, because he is doing this in the name of Jesus. Remember, the disciples had tried to prevent children from getting to Jesus. To receive children "in his name" impels us to relate to children in a righteous manner! Unfortunately today, there are too many weirdoes with other agendas. Incidentally, listen to what Jesus says about those who would harm children or young converts,

"Whoever causes one of these little ones to stumble, it is better for him that a heavy millstone were hung around his neck, and that he was drowned in the depths of the sea" (Matt. 18:6; Mark 9:42). Please note...he is not granting us permission to do this to anyone caught stumbling a child. He merely says, *"it would be better for him* that ..." And without doubt, better for the children too.

Child abuse is an atrocity on whatever level, be it sexual, physical, mental, or abuse by neglect. But amidst the pain of it, Jesus seems to identify himself so closely with these children and childlike that should someone reach out to help them, he would probably say, "As much as you did it to these, you have done it to me!" His actual words were, "Whoever receives one such child in my name, receives me!"

> "Whoever causes one of these little ones to stumble, it is better for him that a heavy millstone were hung around his neck, and that he was drowned in the depths of the sea."

A Real Apprentice

68

If your hand or foot causes you to stumble, cut it off
MATTHEW 18:8; MARK 9:45; LUKE 17:2

Having dealt with the issue of the people who stumble children, with the aid of a very heavy weight and a large ocean, Jesus now gives instruction on how to deal with a stumbling hand or foot! "If your hand or foot causes you to stumble, cut it off and throw it from you." Jesus said so much about healing, but here is a strange alternative view. In the opening pages of this book we considered the controversial command to "sell your coat and buy a sword." Well, there is nothing quite like a sharp sword for disposing of a hand or foot, or dealing with a lusting eye ball! "Pluck it out and cast it from you!" I wonder, do these statements reflect the Lord's sense of humor? The technique of overstatement surely has to be a little tongue in cheek. Or did Jesus actually expect that this command should be practised literally?

> If my eye, hand, or foot is preventing me from getting to heaven, then I would indeed be better off without it. After all, a gangrenous or cancerous foot must be amputated if the rest of the body is to survive.

I admit that I have been known to wield a sharp meat clever while preaching on these verses from the Sermon on the Mount, suggesting that we have a fitting ministry time at the end of the sermon! Can you imagine the mess? There would be piles of offending hands, eyeballs, and stumbling feet outside every church each Sunday! Joking aside, some religions, as you know, do actually practise physical dismembering. Let me emphasize that this "cutting off" as commended by Jesus is something you would inflict upon yourself; thankfully it is not the church leader's responsibility. So, you cut off your own hand if it offends you. I don't cut off your hand if you offend me. A significant difference!!

But does Jesus really mean self-mutilation? Let's just hear it in context: "If your right eye makes you stumble, tear it out and throw it from you; for it is better for you that one of the parts of your body perish than for your whole body to go into hell" (Matt. 5:29). I have never been quite able to identify whether it is my right eye that lusts or whether it's my left one! I suppose I could start by tearing out my right eye, to help me identify which one was at fault … but then I may have unjustly punished the wrong eye! In all honesty, the problem might still continue because the lust actually originated in my mind, not my eyeballs. Perhaps a lobotomy might be needed to sort the problem! However, the threat of losing an eye the next time I lust might just provide sufficient incentive for me to be more disciplined in the future! There is amazing logic in these words of Jesus. If my eye, hand, or foot is preventing me from getting to heaven, then I would indeed be better off without it. After all, a gangrenous or cancerous foot must be amputated if the rest of the body is to survive. (Please seek advice before following this one too literally!! You may want to read the next point first.)

69

If your brother sins, reprove him

MATTHEW 18:15; LUKE 17:3

Perhaps when Jesus talks about cutting off parts of the body he is referring to cutting off offending members of the body of Christ. Can you think of a few offensive people in your church that you would like to see cut off? Seriously, Matthew chapter 18 deals with the problem of sin in the church. Not unlike cancer, if it were left, it could bring death to the body. So Jesus provides a four-pronged strategy to address the issue of offense in the body of Christ:

Firstly, if I see someone sin I must spread the word quickly...the newsletter, or perhaps Facebook, might help, and the church gossip mongers always do a good job! Certainly, the pastor will need to know, and some one-to-one time with the pastor might even score some personal points in the process! Absolutely not, sorry! Such sin should remain a secret, and should be dealt with privately, remaining an issue between the offender and me alone. If he listens to me, I have won my brother. If I mishandle it, I could lose my brother. Certain guidelines are given, such as removing the log from my own eye first; and needing to be spiritual (Gal. 6:1). I may even need to sing a rebuke to the offending person, as in Colossians 3:16: "Admonish one another with psalms, hymns and spiritual songs". This is my preferred option, because my embarrassment of having to sing a rebuke would be greater than that of the person I am reproving, and I am convinced they would not wish to repeat the experience, so would never sin again!

Should this first private approach fail, the second strategy would be to have another person accompany me, "So that by the mouth of two or three witnesses every fact may be confirmed" (v 16). Now the sin is a

> "Admonish one another with psalms, hymns, and spiritual songs."

little less secret, but there is still damage limitation in place. I presume the aim of this exercise is that another person witnesses my attempt to correct my brother, rather than being a witness to his original sin. Difficulties may arise if I need to ask everyone in the church if they are aware, or not aware, of this brother's particular sin! (Unfortunately, some people actually do do this.) Should the offender refuse to capitulate even when other parties enter into the equation, then (and only then) should the third strategy come into play, which is to bring the matter before the church. This must not be considered spiteful or unhelpful—it is designed to increase the pressure with intent to eradicate the sin. Like a thorn in the hand, this sin could ultimately affect the health of the body. If he stubbornly refuses to respond even then, the final option is to treat him like the tax man! Honestly, that is what Jesus said! At this stage the offender should be put out, like the cat, hopefully to be reintroduced again later!

70

If he repents forgive him

LUKE 17:3

This follows on from our last point. Expulsion from fellowship should always assume an openness for a sinner's repentance. Jesus instructs us to treat these brothers as Gentiles or as tax gatherers ... so what would we do with them? I suggest we would evangelize them, seek to invite them to come back on board, and we would explain to them how to repent and receive forgiveness. Well, that is exactly how we should treat an unrepentant brother. And when he does repent? We forgive him.

> Sometimes the painful memories may linger or revisit us from time to time, but that allows us the privilege to forgive all over again!

This should of course be an external demonstration of forgiveness, for we should have already forgiven him in our hearts. In truth, we should forgive even if he fails to repent. An unforgiving spirit puts us in danger of being unforgiven ourselves. (See Mark 11:26), and if that verse is not in your version of the Bible, look at Matthew 6:15. I kid you not, it is missing from some texts! But if this verse were an afterthought, it serves to underline the relative importance placed on this truth by the early Christians who added it.

I have heard some say they will only forgive "as God forgives," and he only forgives when we repent and say that we are sorry. Perhaps that's the way it seems, but actually God has already forgiven us, even before we ask, because our sins were addressed at the cross. God has already dealt with his requirements regarding sin in Christ's death. The price has already been paid in full. It is finished! So forgiveness has already left heaven; we receive it through repentance and confession. The choice is ours whether or not to receive. "If we confess our sins, he is *faithful* and *righteous*, to forgive us our sins and to cleanse us from all unrighteousness" (1 John 1:9 emphasis added). God is *faithful* to his Son who took the punishment for our sins on his shoulders. He is *righteous* because he has no desire to punish twice for the same sins, unless we particularly want to shoulder that penalty ourselves as well. Christ died for sin once and for all. Forgiveness is essential for our own health and happiness. Bitterness and unforgiveness eat into our souls. Sometimes those who have grieved us will never be able to repent or ask our forgiveness. Perhaps someone has caused us pain in the past, but is now long gone, perhaps even dead. They will not ask for our forgiveness, but we give it anyway, and in forgiving we find freedom from the pain and the anger. Sometimes the painful memories may linger, or revisit us from time to time, but that allows us the privilege to forgive all over again! Surely, it is the aim for every disciple to become like Jesus, and exercising forgiveness is the closest we will ever get!

71

Forgive up to seventy times seven

MATTHEW 18:21–22; LUKE 17:4

How many times should we forgive someone who continues to wrong us? The answer is as many times as is necessary—up to four-hundred-and-ninety times! That is seventy times seven, says Jesus, in response to Peter's question as to whether we should forgive the same person as many as seven times. Peter was possibly feeling his own suggestion was completely outrageous, so Jesus's reply must have totally shocked! In other words, the number of times we should forgive is limitless. Actually, I am grateful for Jesus's response, for it demonstrates that God continues to forgive us, even when we persist in making the same mistakes. Our patience in asking for his forgiveness will run out long before his patience in giving it!

As the poet Alexander Pope once wrote, "To err is human but to forgive is divine."[13] Forgiveness presents us with opportunities to emulate God, so we should be glad for every chance to demonstrate this divine quality (Luke 17:4), even if it requires us to forgive the same person seven times in one day for the same transgression. When Jesus said this, the disciple's response was, "Increase our faith" (v 5). I admit that I don't ever recall the need to forgive the same person seven times in one day; however, I am sure some of my readers will remember having to forgive me that often! Seven forgiven offenses a day would seem quite adequate to cover most eventualities. But now imagine having to forgive

156   Graham Warner

> God continues to forgive us, even when we persist in making mistakes. Our patience in asking for his forgiveness will run out long before his patience in giving it!

someone seven times a day for the next ten weeks (seventy days) ... would that stretch one's patience? Yet that is the nature of God's forgiveness.

The presence of the number seven in this equation surely associates it with perfection. It is not just the repetition, but also the quality of this forgiveness that is key. We need to forgive utterly and completely. Listen to how Paul describes it in Colossians 3:13 (MSG): "Be even-tempered, content with second place, quick to forgive an offense. Forgive as quickly and completely as the Master forgave you." And again, in Ephesians 4:32 (MSG), he encourages us to "Be gentle with one another, sensitive. Forgive one another as quickly and thoroughly as God in Christ forgave you." When we have been hurt, it is possible that our bruised emotions might bubble to the surface several times a day, so when they do—forgive! In fact, why not embark on a ten-week course of consciously forgiving such an incident several times a day, until its pain gradually fades into a totally forgiven memory?

72

If you wish to enter into life, keep the commandments

MATTHEW 19:17; LUKE 18:20

I have always found this account in Luke's gospel to be somewhat amusing. Jesus has just explained the necessity to become like a little child in order to enter the kingdom, when a young ruler asks, "But what shall *I* do to inherit eternal life?" (emphasis added) as though he is somehow different from everyone else. He has obviously just heard how the rest of the world must come by humility, but clearly thinks there must be something special he can do to enter the kingdom via his own efforts. So Jesus plays him at his own game by saying, "You know the commandments." The only other way into the kingdom would presumably be via self-perfection—to have never infringed a single law throughout life. As far as the five laws Jesus highlights: "Do not commit adultery, do not murder, do not steal, do not bear false witness, honor your father and mother," he can honestly reply, "I have kept all these since my youth." (It is a little worrying if his murdering and adultery days were as a child but since his youth he has been OK!) But interestingly, Jesus does not mention here the laws concerning relationship with God, such as: "You shall have no other gods before me." Unfortunately, in this department this man fell sadly short. He was wealthy, owning much property, and when asked to surrender his possessions for the sake of the poor, he decided that heaven was not so appealing!

None of us will enter life by observing the commandments. The standards are too high! The children of Israel failed miserably in the Old Testament, and anyone aspiring to achieve the perfection of the Law in the New Testament age would soon discover that the demands are impossibly high. That is why salvation comes through Jesus alone, and why humility is the one and only route. We must admit our failures and weakness, and receive eternal life as a gift from God. However, this does not mean the commandments have no importance. Jesus said, "For truly I say to you, until heaven and earth pass away, not the smallest letter or stroke shall pass from the Law until all is accomplished. Whoever then annuls one of the least of these commandments, and so teaches others to do the same, shall be called least in the kingdom of heaven; but whoever keeps and teaches them, he shall be called great in the kingdom of heaven" (Matt. 5:18-19). The secret to fulfilling these laws is, of course, the Holy Spirit, who lives them out in us. The Old Testament *demanded,* "Thou shalt not!" but the New Testament *promises,* "You will not." Commandments become promises when we have God's Spirit in our heart!

> The Old Testament demanded "Thou shalt not!" but the New Testament promises, "You will not." Commandments become promises when we have God's Spirit in our heart!

A Real Apprentice   159

73

Do not lord it over, whoever wishes to be great must serve

MATTHEW 20:26; MARK 10:43; LUKE 12:26

"You know that the rulers of the Gentiles lord it over them. ...It is not so among you, but whoever wishes to become great among you shall be your servant, and whoever wishes to be first among you shall be your slave; just as the Son of Man did not come to be served but to serve, and to give His life a ransom for many" (Matt. 20:25–28). These verses define the upside down character of the kingdom so brilliantly. I love this whole Jesus principle, that the least become the most important while the first become last. He champions the cause of the underdog, and is a genuine supporter of the weak, the helpless, and the poor. His value system is diametrically opposite to the way the world values people and status. In the world we climb the ladder of success, but in the kingdom of Jesus we must descend the ladder to find success. To discover the place of the very least is to attain the place of greatness!

Jesus links to this concept the command to "not lord it over one another." Greatness in the world's eyes is to be in the position of power; power means authority, and authority means telling people what to do. Not so in his kingdom! Interestingly, Jesus never describes himself as the *king* of the church, but the *head*. A king will rule by external commands, but the head rules the body by internal impulses. A king rules his subjects;

they are his servants. Have you ever considered whether your body serves your head, or your head serves your body? It is actually a reciprocal relationship, where communication flows *both* ways. Unfortunately, the concepts of authority and leadership as modelled by the world are sadly amiss.

> In the world, we climb the ladder of success, but in the kingdom of Jesus we must descend the ladder to find success.

Biblical leadership is all about learning how to serve. Taking authority over people does not even enter into it. Yes, I know there are scriptures which say we should obey the leaders who rule over us (1 Thess. 5:12), but this should more accurately read, *appreciate* the leaders who "stand before" us. In other words, it is their example that we follow. The idea of obedience has to do with "being persuaded" by our leader, rather than having to adhere to his stark dictates whether we like it or not. So a leader should lead by example with one hand, and sensible reasoning with the other. In other words, we follow a leader's instruction because we are truly persuaded by him that a course of action is the right one. That is leadership serving the church with logic, truth, and reasoning. The leader is not the top of the pile; he is the bottom, the foundation…and the servant of all whom he seeks to support!

74

Render unto Caesar the things that are Caesar's

MATTHEW 22:21; MARK 12:17; LUKE 20:25

Here is a brilliant retort by Jesus, in answer to the question, "Is it lawful to pay taxes to Caesar or not?" as we read in the New International Version. You will remember, Jesus asked for a coin and then asked whose inscription and likeness the coin bore. When they replied, "Caesar's," he suggested that they give to Caesar what was Caesar's, and give to God what was God's. Their question was craftily formulated with intent to trap Jesus, for whichever way he had responded the answer would potentially have incriminated him. The Jews believed that the land of Israel had been given to them by God. As far as they were concerned, the Romans had no right to be there, let alone to extract taxes; and so for Jesus to endorse Caesar's poll tax would clearly be a betrayal of their Jewish allegiances. But if Jesus had suggested withholding Roman taxes, the Roman authorities would have been down on him like a ton of bricks. It was indeed a clever trap, but Jesus completely outwitted them with his own unique brand of wisdom. To suggest that Roman coins should be given back to Rome seemed to show compliance with Caesar's tax system—yet it simultaneously supported the Jewish stance (i.e. to oust all that was Roman back to Rome—very, very clever!).

Jesus of course did pay taxes (although quite supernaturally) even though he was legally exempt as an itinerant (Matt. 17:26). Jesus told Peter to go and cast a line into the sea and to open the mouth of the first fish he caught; there he would find a coin with which to pay the taxes.

> This command seems to merely address the legalities of taxation—but, in truth, it poses a much deeper, thought-provoking challenge to give to God what belongs to God.

162   Graham Warner

It was a wonderful miracle and an amazing word of knowledge rolled into one, but the moral was to emphasize that it is fine to pay our taxes. Perhaps I should book a fishing trip before the end of this next tax year!

At face value this command seems to merely address the legalities of taxation—but in truth it poses a much deeper, thought-provoking challenge—to give to God what belongs to God. If Roman coins bear the image of Rome, they belong to Rome. So people, who bear the image of God because they are made in his image, belong to God. What a brilliant challenge! It necessitates that we clarify what belongs where. That which is of the world belongs to the world, but that which belongs to the Lord should be committed to him. The chief priests marvelled at Jesus's wisdom; in fact it silenced them completely! They went home twice the losers, for now they had to pay their money in taxes and also give their lives over to God! I suspect they probably did neither!

Love God with all your heart

MATTHEW 22:37; MARK 12:30; LUKE 10:27

This is the greatest commandment, and the keystone to the fulfilment of the remainder. Perhaps I should have put this right at the start, but here it is three quarters of the way through. It reveals the motivation behind everything that you are reading. The commands of Jesus are not about cold obedience to a New Testament legal system, but the key to relationship; "You are My friends, if you do what I command you" (John 15:14). If you really love someone you want to find ways to please him or her. I was once on a mission project with someone who drove eight hundred miles to make his wife a cup of tea and then drove eight hundred miles back again. That is totally crazy! Yes, but I expect she appreciated the loving sacrifice. Young love is like that—it does crazy things to demonstrate how much it cares for a certain person. I like the encouragement in Revelation 2:4–5 that reminds us when we lose our first love, to go back and do the first works. The first works of love are often the extravagant things that one does to express a love that is head over heels.

All the commands of Jesus give opportunities to express our love and devotion to him, which is why he said, "If you love Me, you will keep My commandments" (John 14:15). Therefore, love is not a feeling, or at least if it starts as a feeling it certainly ends with an action. "God so loved the world that he gave..." (John 3:16). His love is expressed with an action like the giving of his Son. When we are told to love God with all our hearts, it should not just be a heart that is full of emotion, but a heart that is so full that it overflows into loving expressions, active demonstrations, and practical communication—anything that shows, "Lord, I love you." It means our love for Jesus is directly linked to the Jesus of the Gospels. I am not sure that we can really love the Lord, who is seated in majesty on the throne on high, without seeing that he hasn't changed. He is exactly the same yesterday, today, and forever. What he looked for in his devoted followers in the first century is what he looks for today. To love Jesus in heaven is directly proportional to loving the Jesus of the Gospels.

> The commands of Jesus are not about cold obedience to a New Testament legal system but the key to a relationship. If you really love someone, you want to find ways to please them.

One day, it says, all the secrets of our hearts are going to be revealed. Is Jesus the secret of your heart? For where your treasure is there will your heart be also. Jesus described the kingdom to be like treasure hidden in a field, which once discovered, would so captivate us that we would be prepared to sell everything in order to possess it (Matt. 13:44).

76

Love the Lord your God with all your strength

MATTHEW 22:37; MARK 12:30; LUKE 10:27

You shall love the Lord your God with all your soul and with all your strength. These are challenging statements and provoke some thought as to how often we fulfil such commands. Using all our energy and soul in loving God adds a fresh dynamic in expressing and exploring new ways to worship him.

David, as he danced with all his might before the ark of the covenant, provides an example of someone worshipping with all his strength. Some years ago, I recall the worship leader in our church introducing a song, "We Will Dance as David Danced." My brother who was sitting next to me turned and said, "I hope we are not going to dance as David danced," then added, "because he stripped to his underpants!" David did strip down to a linen ephod—and not surprisingly, his wife was a bit upset! Actually, she despised David for shouting and leaping and dancing with all his might in public. But David had humbled himself before the Lord because he esteemed the Lord more than he cared for his own reputation (2 Sam, 6:13–16). He was, as the line of a famous hymn describes, lost in wonder, love, and praise!

> We should work as hard as we can, sing as loud as we can, dance as energetically as we can, serve with all the zeal, eagerness, fervor, passion, and gusto we can muster!

Solomon provides another example when he says, whatever your hands find to do, truly, do it with all your might, because there is no activity, planning, or wisdom beyond the grave (Eccles. 9:10). This life offers us the opportunity to work hard as a form of worship. *Now* is the only time in all eternity that we have to serve Jesus in practical things; we will never get the chance to clean toilets for Jesus in the afterlife, or to get a sweat on our brow serving our earthly bosses, so whatever we do, we must do it wholeheartedly as to the Lord. Let's put our backs into it. Christians should work harder than non-Christians. We should always be happy to go that extra mile, because we have the incentive not just to use our strength but *all* our strength in the service and worship of our Lord. We should work as hard as we can, sing as loudly as we can, dance as energetically as we can, serve with all the zeal, eagerness, fervor, passion, and gusto that we can muster. Love God with all your soul and with all your strength!

77

You shall love the Lord your God with all your mind

MATTHEW 22:37; MARK 12:30; LUKE 10:27

This is an addition to the original text from which Jesus is quoting (Deut. 6:5), which mentions heart, soul, and might only. But in reading the whole context in the Law, the implication is clearly there, "These words, that I am commanding you today shall be on your heart. You shall teach them diligently to your sons and shall talk of them when you sit in your house and when you walk by the way and when you lie down and when you rise up. You shall bind them as a sign on your hand and they shall be as frontals on your forehead. You shall write them on the doorposts of your house and on your gates." (Deut. 6:6-10). God's intention was that the mind should be continually occupied with these things, wherever we go and whatever we are doing.

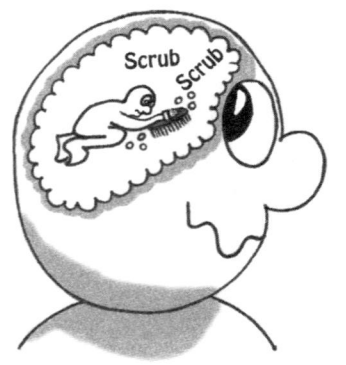

It is one thing to be consciously aware of God's words at all times, but quite another to love God with the whole mind at all times. So vast is the brain that our bodies happily function using approximately three percent of its capacity! For those of us with only a couple of active brain cells it is perhaps easier to completely fulfil this command! The human brain consists of ten thousand million cells, each of which can interconnect, making a staggering amount of possible connections. In fact, if the number were written down it would be one followed by ten million kilometres of standard typewritten noughts—which incidentally, is more than the number of atoms in the entire universe![14] Crumbs! What a challenge to love God with the whole mind.

> The human brain consists of 10,000 million cells, each of which can interconnect, making a staggering amount of possible connections. In fact, if the number were written down it would be 1 followed by 10 million kilometers of standard typewritten noughts.

I love the thought of reprogramming my brain with the information God makes available to us in the Bible. I used to enjoy studying animal behavior, which has been pre-programmed into the brain, and referred to as instinct. God has not programmed us in the same way. He allows us choice. We program our own minds. Yes, this constitutes brainwashing, but it is a voluntary washing of our thought processes with the Word of God. The purpose of Jesus's teaching is to provide the raw material to enable us to think as heavenly beings: conscious and unconscious brain activities become attuned with our maker. Paul puts it like this in Romans 12:2, "Be not conformed to this world, but be transformed by the renewing of your mind, that you may prove what the will of God is, that which is good, acceptable and perfect."

78

You shall love your neighbor as yourself

MATTHEW 22:39; MARK 12:31

If you ask people how many commands Jesus gave to us, the classic answer is to say just two: the first is to love God, and the second is to love your neighbor as you love yourself. It is true that these two commands do embrace all the other commands Jesus gave us, and I hope you are beginning to appreciate the length and breadth of the picture.

This statement is very similar to one we have already considered: Treat others as we would want to be treated, which Jesus also stated summed up all other laws, but this one has something additional to say.

I have often heard these verses used as a reason that it is imperative to love ourselves, because we cannot love our neighbor unless we love ourselves. Allow me to be very controversial by suggesting that this does *not* say "love yourself." Look at it carefully. The words state we should love our neighbor *as* we love ourselves. So quite literally, the good news is that if we don't love ourselves too much, then we don't have to love our neighbor too much! What a relief! I am not a self-lover, so a burden is lifted from my shoulders! But wait a moment—despite the fact that I don't love myself, I still feed and clothe myself, I ensure that I am warm and dry, have a comfortable bed in which to sleep, and a pleasant home in which to live. I have some financial resources in the bank for a rainy day (only one, mind you!)...in fact, considering I don't love myself, I seem to do plenty to ensure my life is pleasant and comfortable. The challenge is—do I do as much for my neighbor? (We will consider the question as to *who* is my neighbor a little later.) But if I find it difficult to love my neighbor even as little as I love myself, imagine the task that is laid at the door of those who really love themselves! If you love yourself greatly, then you must love your neighbor with equal passion: bad news if you are totally self-absorbed, because you must now become equally absorbed in the concerns of your neighbors—actually, I can't help but feel sorry for these poor neighbors! The imperative is clear—we must love our neighbors *as* we love ourselves.

> If we don't love ourselves too much, then we don't have to love our neighbor too much!

Jesus says that loving your neighbor as you love yourself sums up the Law and the Prophets. In fact the whole of the Law and the Prophets rests on this principle (Matt. 22:40).

79

Go and do likewise
(be a Good Samaritan!)

LUKE 10:37

A certain lawyer, wishing to justify himself (we all know solicitors!), asked Jesus, "Who is my neighbor?" He had rightly observed that to love God and your neighbor was the very essence of the Law, but he was seeking some case law to try to understand its application. He needed some kind of personal opt-out clause to justify his selfish living, but unfortunately ended up being challenged by the parable of the Good Samaritan. Probably he lived in a grand house with such extensive grounds that he considered himself to have no neighbors! Jesus turned this story around to ask a different question—not, who is *my* neighbor, but whose neighbor are *you*?

The wounded man in the parable was not this Samaritan's next door neighbor. He was a complete stranger. The challenge presented is whether or not we would be prepared to become the neighbor of a needy stranger. We frown at the priest and are amazed at the indifference of the Levite as they pass by and do nothing, but quite frankly, we probably do likewise, day in and day out. Busyness is our excuse, such as rushing off to church like the priest. He was possibly rehearsing his sermon for that morning's service as he walked by, the title of which was, "Be not contaminated by the world!" Perhaps the hurrying Levite was running late to chair a social action committee meeting and it couldn't start without him! We all have our excuses. (Mine are genuine, of course, otherwise I would stop to help!) We also become embarrassed about involving ourselves when everybody else is passing by. Involvement draws attention, and others look on as if we were some kind of Good Samaritan! Exactly! That's the point! "Lord, give me boldness to cross the street and get involved, and give me a love that is greater than my own self-consciousness." Jesus told another parable that was in a way about crossing the street. It has become known as Lazarus and the Rich Man. Lazarus had lain at the rich man's gate in absolute poverty, the dogs licking his sores, until death. The rich man who had lived sumptuously died too. Suddenly, the tables had

> "Lord, give me boldness to cross the street and get involved, and give me a love that is greater than my own self-consciousness."

turned—Lazarus had now "entered into good things," but the rich man was suffering and a great gulf existed between them. That great gulf had actually been present during their lifetime, but the rich man had refused to cross it to meet the beggar's need (Luke 16:19–26). Today's challenge—cross a gulf and become a neighbor to someone!

80

Do what they say, do not do what they do

MATTHEW 23:3

We are already aware of a warning from Jesus to "beware of the teaching of the Pharisees" and here Jesus raises the subject again, but this time, believe it or not, he suggests that the Pharisees sometimes have useful things to say! And on the rare occasions when they do, we should do what they say. So, sometimes even the Pharisees had correct theory—if only they had endeavored to live by it. It is bad enough to believe one thing and do another, but even worse to teach others to do something with no intention of following one's own advice.

> God does lift his finger to help us! The Lord never lays a burden upon us that he does not intend to carry himself.

Jesus describes the teaching of the Pharisees as "tying up heavy burdens and laying them on men's shoulders" while refusing to lift a finger to assist those crushed by the load! To me this resembles preaching that appears to be full of Biblical truth, yet somehow ministers death! I can remember attending churches where I entered with faith but came out with none—ministries using Biblical truth to actually strangle life and increase guilt, with a slice of condemnation thrown in for good measure. Alright, I hear what you say—it's just like this book! If you are reeling under the weight of these impossible commands, you need to notice that Jesus breathes hope and life, even into a deadly Pharisaical sermon. "Do what they say." But isn't this too heavy a burden? Even if it is, we can still do it. As long as it is truth, and if the Holy Spirit empowers us, the Lord can enable us to live a life beyond the expectations and teachings of the Pharisees, and our righteousness will exceed theirs. Why? Because God does lift his finger to help us! The Lord *never* lays a burden upon us that he does not intend to carry himself. When God says something, he also does it himself. And what God says to us he also does in us, by his Holy Spirit. Unlike the Pharisees, God is true to his word. He honors his word above his name, and will always fulfil his promises.

"Do not according to their deeds" is the other exhortation given in these verses. The apostle Paul would use himself as the example when he taught, "You know my manner of life" or "knowing from whom you have learned these things." His lifestyle gave credibility to his message. That is an element of the fruit that we considered earlier. But we can still learn something from a Pharisee, even if he has a disappointing lifestyle. Wisdom says you can listen to the rebuke of a fool and still become wiser (Prov. 15:32)!

A Real Apprentice 175

81

Do not be called teacher/father/leader

MATTHEW 23:8–10

Oops! Here is a triplet of commands of which we seem to fall foul: "Do not be called **teacher**," "Do not be called **father**," and "Do not be called **leaders**" (emphasis added). I feel sorry for *Father* Brown, the *leader* of the local church, who is the *teacher* every Sunday. Surely, he has infringed some significant commands here? Are some of our religious establishments breaking these golden rules by the titles given to their personnel?

These statements actually refer to misuse of position and status, *not* to a function being performed. Examples of correct usage would be in Paul's observation, "You have not many *fathers*," where he was clearly referring to himself as their father: then there is a gift of *teacher* given to the church in Ephesians 4:11; and Romans 12:8 exhorts that those who *lead* should do it with all diligence. Here are three functions that operate quite legitimately within any church, so what then is the point Jesus made? Perhaps the context reveals some clues, because the preceding verses describe the way the Pharisees loved places of honor at banquets and respectful greetings in the market squares. They loved to be called Rabbis, and even wore extravagant religious clothing so that they would be noticed. This seems to identify the problem: Jesus spoke out against those who were full of their own importance and those who felt they were superior to the rest! Hence, Jesus explained, "Do not be called Rabbi; for One is your Teacher and you are all brothers" (Matt. 23:8). This highlights two specific things. One is that the Lord is our teacher and that we can go straight to him to be taught—we do not necessarily need an intermediary. (It is not that teachers are unhelpful. They certainly are able to help, but we should not become overly reliant on them, as though they are the only way to hear from God.) This teaching began by saying, "The scribes and Pharisees have seated themselves in the chair of Moses" (v 2). They had set themselves up as the mediators between God and men. If we were unable to access our heavenly Father because we had been taught that the only way to reach him was through an earthly father, then our personal relationship with the Lord would have been lost. The same applies to leaders—if we could only be led and guided by men called leaders, we would stop seeking to be led by The Great Shepherd himself. The other area highlighted follows on quite naturally, that is to say, we are all brothers and therefore all equal in God's sight; a brother may serve as a leader, but he is on the same plain as everyone else, equal brothers together.

> The Lord is our teacher and we can go straight to him to be taught—we do not necessarily need an intermediary.

82

Don't neglect the law of, justice, mercy, and faithfulness
MATTHEW 23:23

Hypocrites seem to have an uncanny way of majoring on minor issues. Jesus sums up such pettiness as "straining on a gnat but swallowing a camel." The Pharisees had a tendency to focus on insignificant details while completely missing the point. Such was their attention to detail that even the herbs growing in their gardens were included in their tithing! They "tithe mint, dill and cumin" (Matt. 23:23), while ignoring the weightier laws about justice, mercy, and faithfulness. It is not that minor things should be totally ignored, although I must confess I have never even considered tithing the flowers, herbs, and fruits which grow in my garden. Have you? Perhaps that is precisely why the Pharisees labored such points; it gave them some kind of power over others, engendering not just guilty feelings, but also admiration on account of their thoroughness.

However, Jesus was not impressed and could see through their pretense. These outwardly righteous men were inwardly full of hypocrisy and lawlessness. They would criticize the plucking of a grain or two on the Sabbath, but think nothing of plotting to kill a man. Behind their loud and lengthy prayers, and seemingly righteous exterior, lurked murderous hearts. They admitted to being sons of those who had killed

---

All the laws are important, but Jesus shows us that some are more important than others.

---

the prophets, but justified themselves by denying that they would have been party to such actions: meanwhile they were busy calculating how to rid themselves of the Son of God! Little wonder then that Jesus called them "serpents, a brood of vipers." The Pharisees were supposed to be authorities on judgment and justice. Their function was to defend the poor and the fatherless, to look after the interests of the needy and afflicted. They should, therefore, have been the epitome of mercy and faithfulness. The temple should have been a place for love and forgiveness—but they turned it into a den of thieves, full of greed, extortion, criticism, and condemnation.

All the laws are important, but Jesus shows us that some are more important than others. We need to obey them all, while giving extra precedence to the weightier issues. If you were to apply a scoring system, allocating marks out of ten to each of these life principles, how closely matched would they be to Jesus's value system?

83

Do not be troubled by wars and rumors

MATTHEW 24:6; MARK 13:7; LUKE 21:9

It is difficult to watch an evening news program without sensing the fulfilment of the words of Jesus regarding end times—particularly the prediction that iniquity would abound (literally "super-abound") and that evil would overflow the banks. Suicide bombers target and indiscriminately kill en masse; terrorism is becoming an everyday threat; there is a remarkable rise in the number of natural disasters such as earthquakes, tsunamis, hurricanes, tornadoes, floods, and storms; nations are at war, with others threatening war—the world is becoming an increasingly insecure place. But Jesus, having predicted all this, says in essence, "When you see it—do not be afraid! For these things must take place, but the end is not yet" (Matt. 24:6).

Yesterday, that is the day before writing this page, my wife and I toured the Nazi death camps at Auschwitz in Poland. We viewed the place where eight thousand Jews were killed each day—day after day, women and children, and the weakest of the men. Over three million people in all were led like lambs to the slaughter, believing they were being led into showers, but instead were showered with lethal pellets of Cyclon B gas. We stood in a square where five thousand people were shot by firing squad. But strangely they were the lucky ones! For hundreds of thousands more died slow, lingering deaths, through starvation and exhaustion, in the labor camps: man's incredible inhumanity to man! One slogan on the wall read, "So long as we don't forget, this will never happen again!" We did, and it does! Unfortunately it has happened again and again with horrific cases of ethnic cleansing ... to say nothing of tyrants like Pinochet, Gadaffi, Saddam Hussein, Osama Bin Laden and Bashar al-Assad, and yet these things are probably just a pale shadow of things yet to come. This is the ugliest face of the worst in the world, inspired by the darkness of the dark kingdom of Satan. The forces of hell will release their fury as time draws to a close, but Jesus's encouragement

> Where darkness has been at its darkest, there the brightest light will shine, so these dark days will actually be great days of evangelism.

is twofold: (1) Do not be afraid and (2) "This gospel shall be preached in the whole world for a testimony to all the nations, and then the end will come" (Matt. 24:14). Where darkness has been at its darkest, there the brightest light will shine, so these dark days will actually be great days of evangelism; amidst all the hopelessness, the gospel of hope shall shine. If we feel the days are getting darker, we need to be on the offensive with the message of Christ. The quicker we accomplish the task, the sooner we hasten the day and wrap up depressing world history.

84

Care for the poor and needy

MATTHEW 25:35-37

The *poor and needy* mentioned in this passage are defined as the hungry, the thirsty, the stranger, the naked, the sick, and the prisoner. Some would say that these verses describe imperatives for the nations (see verse 32) rather than for individuals. I don't mind this interpretation, because it excuses me from personal involvement and responsibility. The Pharisees and I have much in common with regard to finding loopholes—this alternative interpretation means I don't need to apply these difficult challenges to myself. So this could be a description of God's judgment of national policies.

It has also been said that the poor and needy in these verses could be Jews, as the term, "these brethren," is used to describe the recipients of the care; so this could possibly refer to national policy regarding Israel. Or even better, the brethren could mean the church! Now we're getter somewhere—this could be, after all, about me ! I don't have to serve the poor—I am the poor! This could actually be a description of God's judgment of the nations' policies towards the church. After all, Christ is in me, so if the nations feed and clothe me, it is as if they are doing so for Christ. That's it! I don't have to care for the poor, and even better, I just sit back while others seek to care for me! Great!

If all that were true, I can't help but feel there might yet be a challenge in this for me. If the Lord expects such levels of care for the poor from non-Christian nations, does he expect any less from me? Would I be any less excluded from caring for fellow brethren, whether they be Jews or Christians? And what if this were Jesus actually identifying himself with genuinely poor people out there in the world, and that the word "brethren" refers to "fellow man"? After all, all mankind is made in the image of God. If we neglect the image, are we not showing neglect for the one behind the image, that is the Lord? If I gave you my photograph and you promptly placed it under your foot and ground my face into the mud, I would probably think you didn't like me too much! What you do to my image shows what you think of me. What if grinding the face of the poor into the mud actually offends Christ? These verses define those wishing to be in the group called the "righteous." Righteousness has a duty of care: to feed those that are hungry, to satisfy the thirst of the thirsty, to look after the stranger, to visit those who are sick, to clothe those who are naked, and to visit those who are in prison. This is a challenge to practical social action. It may mean getting involved with people that are sometimes not very nice! So, how should we treat unsavory characters with unpleasant odors? As if they were Jesus himself!

> It may mean getting involved with people that are sometimes not very nice—unsavory characters with unpleasant odors.

85

Give what is in the plate as charity

LUKE 11:41

This rather cryptic statement is one in a series of denigrating criticisms of the Pharisees which we considered earlier. "They clean the outside of the cup and the platter, but inwardly they are full of robbery and wickedness." And now Jesus adds, "Give what is within as charity and all will be clean for you." The picture that springs to mind is that of a collection plate; one can imagine the Pharisees rubbing their hands in glee as they watch the "hilarious givers" in the synagogue responding to the rabbi's teaching on tithing (everything down to the garden herbs!). *Everything in this plate is ours*, they think ... then Jesus ruins their moment by suggesting that everything in the plate be given as charity. "What!" ...a nervous hesitation... "What- err, what a jolly good idea!" the Pharisees reply, with absolutely no intention of putting

> It is revealing that 90% of Jesus' instructions about giving refer to giving to the poor. Nowadays, 90% of our appeals relate to giving to the church!

this money anywhere other than in their own pockets. After all, they loved money (see Luke 16:14). What a shame, because Jesus was offering them an opportunity to become clean.

I wonder how many churches today would react in a similar way should the Lord require that they give away as charity the storehouse of collected tithes? Jesus has an uncanny way of putting his finger right on the button, doesn't he? It is revealing that 90 percent of Jesus's instructions about giving refer to giving *to the poor*. Nowadays 90 percent of our appeals relate to giving *to the church*—which is ultimately nothing more than giving to ourselves!

Jesus seems to use the act of giving to the poor as a means of cleansing the soul. Judas clearly missed this opportunity. He took care of their community finances, but probably helped himself more than he gave to the poor. However, there were others who took it, like Zaccheus, and of course there were those who did not, such as the rich young ruler. Notice that Jesus never suggested that people should channel their giving into the "Jesus expense account," nor did he specify which good cause or charitable organization to support. He leaves it to the initiative of each challenged individual. It saddens me to hear of churches that demand that their members take a serious approach to giving, yet when people respond by giving generously, those who then administer the funds do so in a spirit which is nothing short of miserly! Thank God for the wonderful exceptions to this rule that set an example in generosity!

86

Take, eat, this is my body
MATTHEW 26:26; MARK 14:22; LUKE 22:19; JOHN 6:53

Jesus was an expert at using pictures and symbols—none better known than the bread and wine—bread, the symbol of his body, and wine, the representation of his blood. As usual, he took everyday items and used them to denote some spiritual truth or other. To me this is precisely the point of breaking bread—bread itself is an everyday item. Dare I say that we have probably over-formalized something which Jesus intended to be very informal? He instituted this rite at a supper, which was an informal meal with his friends, and took elements that would have been common to any meal, asking that they would remember him with these things.

I am sure that the early church must have had large, formal Communion services much as we do today, but the descriptions in the book of Acts suggest a kind of informal approach. They broke bread "from house to house" and ate their meals "with gladness of heart" (Acts 2:46). The early church was described as continuing in the apostles' doctrine, fellowship, breaking of bread, and prayers (Acts 2:42). The word *continuing* gives the impression of non-stop activity. I fail to believe that they only enjoyed fellowship on Sundays, or only prayed at weekends; they presumably practiced these throughout the week. Following the apostles'

Could the Lord actually care more about how we
treat the needy than he does about how we worship him?

---

teaching would certainly not have been classified as a part-time activity! So when they continued in the breaking of bread it seems to give the impression that it was an activity which took place more than just a once week, or once a month. I wonder whether Jesus intended us to remember him at every meal, as we eat bread together. I know this is a pernicious doctrine because it presumes that we drink wine on a regular basis. Actually they probably did. Non-alcoholic of course! Or was it?

I have always been amused by the fact that this ceremony became known as the "breaking of bread." It could so easily have become known as "the drinking of wine" service—and you can imagine where that would have led! But seriously, this gives us a wonderful prompt to feed on Christ day by day, and to be ever grateful for his sacrifice on our behalf. It is a reminder that we need his forgiveness and cleansing, however often we practice this particular piece of symbolism. I have perhaps been a little controversial here (quite deliberately), so I apologize! So, let me say again, I am also sure they must have practiced Communion in their church services in much the same way as we do today as well.

87

Go into all the world

MATTHEW 28:19

Jesus leaves some of his greatest challenges until last. I suppose that fits with the stance that the last shall be first! I have described these challenges as *great* because they appear in what has become known as "The Great Commission." Over the next few pages we will examine various aspects of this commission, but we start with the mandate to *go into the world*. We often adopt a *"come* to us" philosophy, where we put a church in the middle of a community and expect non-Christians to *come* and join us. I was brought up teetotal, as are all good Brethren. The first time I entered a pub I felt like a fish out of water. I had gone there to evangelize, and drank only a soft drink—of course! (I have since discovered that Jesus probably drank wine of the alcoholic kind!) I confess that I felt really uncomfortable—almost as if I had found myself behind enemy lines. But it was a good learning experience, because this is exactly how the unchurched feel entering one of our services. I am glad Jesus delivered his message mostly on the streets rather than in the synagogues.

People could feel comfortable around him because the surroundings were familiar. But I think there is more to this *go* strategy. You will remember that Matthew 10:7 said *go*, and as you go preach the message that heaven is here, cast out demons, etc. This indicates a twofold strategy: firstly, to go into the world with the aim to push out darkness, be it demons, death, or illness; and secondly, to release the kingdom of Jesus, the light, the healing, the freedom, etc! So, as we go, we actually change the world, the very environment where non-Christians live! Pushing out Satan's kingdom and allowing the kingdom of heaven to flow in makes the world a better place for everybody. This will only happen when church members enter the world's domain, outside the four walls of church. To be honest, the Lord is probably more interested in what happens around our churches than in the religious games we play inside the four walls of church. So *go* is the mandate, and Jesus taught us to ask to be sent out as laborers; these same words may also be literally translated as "cast out"—as in "casting out" demons—so the church needs to be cast out. And as we are pushed out into the community, we cast out everything associated with the Devil as we go.

> To be honest, the Lord is probably more interested in what happens around our churches than in the religious games we play inside the four walls of the church.

There are millions of people who will never voluntarily walk into a church building, so they will never hear the message of Christ unless we go out to meet them where they are. "As my Father has sent Me even so send I you" (John 20:21).

88

Make disciples of all nations

MATTHEW 28:19

The next section of the Great Commission defines the parameters of the task. We must go into the *whole* world—that is, to every nation, in fact to every ethnic group—with the aim of making disciples in each of them. The book of Revelation records that vast crowds will worship before the throne in heaven. They have come from every nation, tribe, people, and tongue, which is indicative of the church's success in fulfilling the task of world evangelization (Rev 7:9). Luke's record of the Great Commission differs slightly from Matthew and Mark's in that it states *it is written* that "Repentance and forgiveness of sins should be proclaimed in His name to all the nations, beginning in Jerusalem." In other words, *it has already been recorded* that a generation to come should accomplish the task, and when this happens, the end will probably come. Why not make this our generation? What a challenge! We could wrap up world history in our lifetime. We often say it is a small world. Well, let's prove it and take this great gospel out into this tiny planet.

Note the instruction to *make disciples* of all nations. This is the phrase that has provided the inspiration for this book. There is a definitive assignment to be accomplished; we are not just giving out tickets for heaven, to make converts: the brief is to turn converts into disciples, then help them to make more disciples. We have already discussed what is entailed in making a disciple—simply by observing *everything* that he has commanded. That is a clearly definable, manageable undertaking, but sadly, one which the church has been extremely slack in fulfilling.

My hope is that this book will aid apprenticeship in the adventure of following Jesus. For those of us who have been on the road for some

> Making a disciple…that is a clearly definable, manageable undertaking, but sadly, one which the church has been extremely slack in fulfilling.

time, it is good to go back to our roots and remind ourselves why we signed up…rather like a marriage refresher course! The book has been designed as a 101 day program for personal discipleship, but is also an excellent tool for group discussion. After all, the focus of this command is not ourselves: we should be teaching *others* to follow Christ's commands. Why not use this book to disciple others? There are group discussion notes available on my website: www.grahamwarner.com. To be really pedantic, there is no instruction here to *obey* these things—just teach others to do them! You might wish to use this logic as an excuse. Here is another loophole, should you need one! But why not use this book to encourage someone else into real discipleship?

89

Baptize them in the name of the Father, Son, and Holy Spirit

MATTHEW 28:19

Baptism is yet another piece of picture language which beautifully defines what is involved in becoming a Christian, and marks the making of a disciple. (Because I believe in baptism by total immersion, I shall relate my comments to this, so if you come from a different tradition you may need to translate this thinking.) Most traditions baptize in the name of the Father, and of the Son, and of the Holy Spirit. From this statement we can establish the definition of a Christian. He is a person completely immersed in the Father, and in the Son, and in the Holy Spirit: a disciple makes a total commitment to the total Godhead! In this book we are emphasizing the concept of being soaked in Jesus, but Jesus leads us on into relationship with his Father. What a fantastic thought—to be completely baptized into our Father in heaven! In the same way, the Holy Spirit leads us on into understanding and remembering Jesus's words, as well as empowering us to fulfil them. We need to be immersed, baptized, soaked, and ever filled with the Holy Spirit!

The baptism picture shows us so much more: it is a demonstration of burial and resurrection. We died in Christ, and affirm that belief by going to our own funeral. We are laid under the water (probably not six feet under, and not for very long), but quite enough to symbolize the end of our old lives. Then we are raised victoriously into new life! It is as though we are born again!

Baptism also symbolizes an internal washing. Paul was told in Acts 22:16 to arise and be baptized and wash away his sins. The water has no power to cleanse from sin, any more than the river Jordan could have washed away Naaman's leprosy—but by faith Jesus cleanses in the process of this simple action. Yes, I don't doubt that biblically, it was actually during baptism that forgiveness was attained. Today we rarely use baptism as a means of leading some into a commitment to Christ, as seems to have been the case Biblically. For example, Acts 2:38 says, "Repent, and each of you be baptized in the name of Jesus *for the forgiveness of your sins*; and you will receive the gift of the Holy Spirit" (emphasis added). Personally, I think this is a command for us all, so we should all have the privilege of baptizing someone. In practice, I have encouraged those involved in a person's journey to Christ to be involved in their baptism too. But, sadly, this is all too often reserved for leaders alone. I have often amusingly quipped—how could we have got a rite so wrong?!

> A disciple makes a total commitment to the total Godhead!
> Completely immersed in the Father, in
> the Son, and in the Holy Spirit.

90

Don't take the best seats

LUKE 14:8

Should we take the best seats for ourselves? No! In fact, quite the opposite is true. We should always take the lowest place. This was Jesus's response as he observed guests seeking out the places of honor at a wedding feast. With one simple statement he contradicted the spirit of a self-seeking world. The way of the world is to claw one's way to the top, whereas Jesus invites us to claw our way to the bottom. If there were just two seats available—the best and the worst—it is natural that we should want to choose the best for ourselves. The problem is one of value: it would appear that we need to be in a place of honor in order to feel good about ourselves. We naturally enjoy the status and kudos of being revered by humankind; but God values and reveres those who take the *lowest* place.

Our stay at the bottom should nevertheless be short, for when the host of the feast observes our humility, he will invite us to take a place with more honor. In my case, it is usually the person sitting next to me who is exalted, and I remain on my own (and suddenly *very* lonely), in the lowest place! Seriously, there is an important principle here: if we humble ourselves we will be exalted, and if we exalt ourselves we will be humbled. Wherever we finish the day, our task is to start the day seeking the lowest place, and to allow God to exalt us!

I was once invited to a mayor's banquet—with unallocated seating—

so being one of the first to arrive, I had to choose a table and chair. Whilst sipping preprandials and filing into the dining area, I was recounting the tale of the wedding feast to those around me; at the same time I scanned the room to work out where to sit. Finally, having decided that the grand table in the bay window must be the one reserved for the VIPs, I suggested that we take the lowest place, on the table at the opposite side of

> If you humble yourself you will be exalted, and
> if you exalt yourself you will be humbled.

the room. I had just reached the point in the story where Jesus said it would be disgraceful to be asked to surrender your place for a more honorable guest, when Security came and asked me why I was sitting in the mayor's seat. Oops! In disgrace I ended up sitting in the bay window! But I did try!

91

Invite the poor, crippled, lame, and blind when you give a meal

LUKE 14:12–14, 21

This imperative represents the latter half of a two-part command, which begins by saying, "When you give a luncheon or a dinner, do not invite your friends or your brothers or your relatives or rich neighbors." So, it is quite Biblical to ignore some of your relatives if you so wish (what a useful verse!). Actually, I don't think Jesus's intention is that we cease associating with friends and family; he is simply making the observation that if we invite friends, brothers, relatives, or wealthy neighbors, they are likely to return the favor, and so we will receive repayment for our kindness. This command speaks about rewards—if we wish to be eternally rewarded, then we must extend hospitality to those *unable* to return the compliment, such as the poor, the lame, the disabled, and the blind.

This idea is in sympathy with the giving of the cup of cold water mentioned earlier: the Lord rewards every act of kindness, especially sharing our food and our homes with the less fortunate. Hopefully, we enjoy providing hospitality anyway—but the Lord adds his own repayment by way of additional incentive. "For you will be repaid at the resurrection of the righteous." He remembers every charitable deed—which we may have quickly forgotten—and he rewards each one, thereby adding to the wealth of treasure stored up in heaven for each benefactor.

Paul describes such rewards as building with gold, silver, and precious stones, which not only survive the flames of Christ's presence but become refined and purified by it (1 Cor. 3:12–15). Catering for relatives and rich neighbors who repay us presumably falls into the category of building with wood, hay, and stubble—which will ultimately be consumed in the blaze of Christ's glory. My fear is that when I stand before Jesus in judgment, my life will disappear into a little pile of ashes. I can imagine scraping them together and presenting them to the Lord—"This is my life that was!"

> We must extend hospitality to those unable to return the compliment, such as the poor, the lame, the disabled, and the blind.

Jesus encourages us to live with heaven as our focus and to go out into the highways and byways, compelling them to come in. It is perhaps relatively easy to find a poor person, but when was the last time you invited the lame, the disabled, or the blind for a meal?

92

Make friends by using money

LUKE 16:9

Luke 16:1—13 recounts a seemingly difficult story to understand. An irresponsible servant had squandered his master's possessions, and as a consequence was to lose his job. He therefore decided to make some friends, hoping that they might take care of him afterwards. His strategy for making friends was to ask each one how much he owed to his master; then he considerably reduced each debt. Although this seems a little dishonest, the master actually congratulated him for his wisdom. In essence this story is very simple. Jesus explains it in verse 9: "I say to you, make friends for yourselves by the means of the mammon of unrighteousness." Basically, he is suggesting that it is good to use money for making friends.

This is not to say we should be seeking to purchase friendship, but it is perfectly acceptable—good stewardship—to spend money on non-Christians. (This will make church treasurers shudder, because they would prefer this money to find its way into the general fund.) When God sees us using our resources well—and part of that is using money for relationships—he commends us as faithful, and when we are faithful with physical wealth, he will entrust to us true spiritual riches. So, we should consider how we might allocate some of our budget for furthering new friendships—or better still, somebody else's budget, as in the story!

This verse concludes with a cryptic remark, "so that you will be welcomed into eternal dwellings." One can only surmise that these new friends will become converted on account of our kindnesses, and will stand and welcome us into heaven when the time arrives. So ... it is definitely worth being generous with our worldly riches—go on, buy the next round of drinks, throw that party, settle that restaurant bill, or pay the green fees at the golf club. It is good to lend and good to give. I think you probably get the point!

Perhaps all this seems to be rather insignificant—but Jesus says he will make us faithful with much if we are faithful with little (v 10). This command is therefore more than just a good idea to take or leave. It concerns an essential use of the little thing called money. Let's be free with it! We cannot serve God and money (v 13), so we must use some of our money to serve God by serving friendships!

> Buy the next round of drinks, throw that party, settle that restaurant bill, or pay the green fees at the golf club.
> It is good to lend and good to give.

93

Don't say four more months and then harvest

JOHN 4:35

Farmers would say there should be a certain number of months before harvest if the grain or fruit is to be sufficiently ripe—but this is not so with the fruit of the kingdom: the fields are already ripe for harvest. Earlier we looked at Matthew 10, where Jesus says that the harvest is always plentiful. It is continually ripe and ready, and the Lord is continually looking for laborers. "Do not say four months" was a warning to those who would procrastinate, who either refused to believe that the harvest was ripe, or did not feel ready to personally respond. "Don't put off to tomorrow what can be done today" is a familiar expression, which can be readily applied to God's agenda. Do it now! Don't delay! This is the most effective way to get things done. Should we postpone for whatever reason, the *right* moment may never come. What we don't do now, we are unlikely to do later.

Perhaps it is my theological view of God that makes me believe each moment is special, because I think God enjoys the *"now* moment." Time is our most valuable resource. Who knows whether an opportunity will present itself again, or whether it is lost forever? Carpe Diem—seize the day! *Now* is the day of his salvation, *now* is the acceptable time (2 Cor. 6:2). Jesus said, "We must work the works...while it is day, for the night comes when no man can work" (John 9:4). He also said, "My Father is working until *now* and I myself am working" (John 5:17 emphases added).

Making the most of each day is a philosophy prompted by the suspense of the second coming of Christ. He always intended to keep us on the edge of our seats. We have no means of knowing whether there will be an opportunity in four months' time: the only real certainty is today. The servants who thought they had time on their hands because their

> Do it now! Don't delay!
> Don't put off to tomorrow what can be done today.

master was delayed were caught unawares, but the wise virgins with their lamps trimmed were ready. The virgins set the example for us to follow—we must be prepared for the bridegroom's sudden arrival. If you knew that there was no tomorrow, how would you live today? Well, that is how you should live! Jesus related a story about a wealthy man who intended to pull down his barns and build bigger ones, taking the view that he had "many goods laid up for many years" so he could take it easy, eat, drink and be merry (Luke 12:16–21). The Lord replied that he was a tad foolish, because his soul would be required that very night. You never know if there will be a tomorrow—so do it *now*!

94

Wait until you receive power from on high

LUKE 24:49

Having said, "Do it now," I am going to contradict myself by following it with the principle "Wait until you receive power from on high." In some ways it would be pertinent to think that this command applied only to the disciples of the day, rather than for all time, as they were receiving orders to wait for Pentecost before launching out in mission. But the principle must be just as important for us today. The difference is we don't need to wait for forty days. Once the day of Pentecost had arrived, the Holy Spirit was poured out on all flesh, and is now instantly available to be appropriated for action.

This concept is not so much about delaying, then, but making sure that we don't move out in our own strength. If we are going to make the most of each day, we need to work in the power of the Spirit. The Lord can accomplish in moments what for us could take months, so why bother to strive in our own strength? He can provide sushi for five thousand people in a moment (Well, was the fish cooked or not!?), or the choicest Claret in an instant from gallons of foot-washing water! He caused a woman with a hemorrhage to recover in seconds instead of years, and was able to change Saul/Paul's thinking in one stroke by supernatural revelation that endless arguments would never had accomplished. So, wait on the Lord!

Jesus did nothing unless the Father did it through him. If anyone could do things in his own strength, certainly Jesus could. After all, everything was created by him, nothing exists without him—and yet he lived in utter dependence upon his Father. When the early church received power from heaven, three thousand people were converted to Christianity in one day. Now that's powerful! We need to examine ourselves as to how we live. Are we living in the realm of real power or just getting by on our own resources? I have heard it suggested that the church could continue to perform 95 percent of its activities without the

> He can provide sushi for five thousand people in a moment, or the choicest claret in an instant out of gallons of foot-washing water!

involvement of the Holy Spirit. What a very sad indictment! But how would I assess my personal life? What percentage of my daily activities could I do without the power of the Holy Spirit? Actually, I feel as though I am dependent upon him for everything, so perhaps a better question would be "How much supernatural power do I release in the course of a week?" This week? Not enough!

95

Do not marvel, all in the tombs shall hear his voice

JOHN 5:28

If you were to flick through the pages of the Gospels in my Bible you would see many "A.S." entries in the margins. I have written them next to any remarkable statement that Jesus made about himself—A.S. stands for "Amazing Statement." For example, John 8:56 quotes Jesus as saying, "Abraham rejoiced to see my day and he saw it and was glad." Verse 58 states, "Before Abraham was I am." Earlier in the same chapter, verse 23, Jesus states, "You are from below, I am from above; you are of this world, I am not of this world." He makes many similar statements (perhaps material for another book some time!), but here is the one we have before us, "Do not marvel at this; for an hour is coming, in which all who are in the tombs shall hear his voice, and shall come forth."

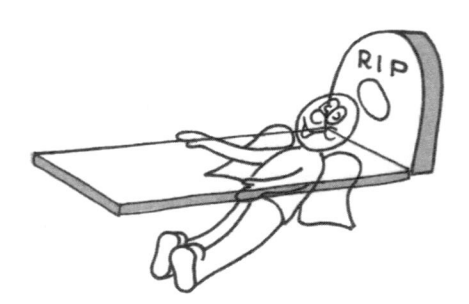

Throughout his teaching, Jesus constantly let slip his true identity. He claims to be the "Resurrection and the Life," and that anybody believing in him would never die—but even if they did die, they would still live forever (John 11:25). He also claims to have "all authority in heaven and on earth." To claim to have all authority on earth is quite some assertion, but to declare that you have all authority in heaven as well is phenomenal! (Matt. 28:18). He also says that "all judgment" has been given to him (John 5:22). He will judge the whole world, and even declares that the world will be judged by the words which he has already spoken (John 12:48)—hence this book. His words have not only played their part in shaping history, they also shape our lives today, and they will also form the basis of our future judgment. His teaching forms the yardstick

> ...The 'Resurrection and the life,' and that anybody believing in him would never die—but even if they did die, they would still live forever.

by which we will be judged. In fact, prior to Jesus's uttering of our title statement about the dead hearing his voice, he confirmed that his Father had given him authority to exercise judgment because he is the Son of Man. How *amazing* are all these statements? And yet Jesus says, "Do not marvel at this!" We should not be surprised; we should expect these kinds of revelations to come shining through—after all, Jesus is *God* in a human body. Without doubt, anyone seriously trying to discover his real identity will find statements of his divinity at every turn, and yet he never boasts about who he is. Self-glory is of no worth, he says in John 8:54, so although we see glimpses of self-revelation everywhere, he leaves it to God the Father to glorify the Son—and he does so all the time! The day is coming when Jesus will speak, and all the dead will hear and come forth out of death! Never was such a thing said about any other person.

96

Do not work for food that perishes

JOHN 6:27

Do not work for the food which perishes, but for the food which endures to eternal life, which the Son of Man shall give to you, for on him the Father, even God, has set his seal." There we are—another A.S. for the margin! This one underlines the fact that the Father glorifies the Son. The seal speaks of God's authority and approval, so Jesus is being marked out among all men as someone totally unique.

> This command is about sorting out our priorities. We should not waste time on things that are unimportant.

This command is about sorting out our priorities. We should not waste time on things that are unimportant. It is fine to work, but we should not work for food that perishes. "Food that perishes" may be defined as leftover food, or food which is superfluous to requirements. So perhaps Jesus is suggesting that we shouldn't work for more than we need. Whilst we shouldn't waste time and energy building up stocks that will never be needed (for they will just rot with time, moth, and rust, etc.), it is acceptable to work for the food we do need. But better still, we should work for food that is eternal.

Jesus can provide us with food that never becomes stale or rots—food that will last forever. He had just fed the multitudes with five loaves, but that was not the kind of bread to which he was referring; he did, however, want them to chew on his teaching. "Man shall not live on bread alone, but on every word that proceeds out of the mouth of God" (Matt. 4:4). Jesus's words are timeless and as fresh today as when he first spoke them. They feed the soul with spiritual food that will endure into eternal life. He is the food that never perishes —"I am the bread of life; he who comes to Me shall not hunger"—he says in verse 35. "My Father who gives you the true bread out of heaven. For the bread of God is that which comes down out of heaven, and gives life to the world" (vv 32–33). In fact this statement is repeated eight times in this one dialogue between verses 32 and 58. He who eats this bread shall live forever! Work for food that does not perish. This work, says Jesus, means to simply believe in him, "This is the work of God that you believe in Him whom He has sent" (v 29). Jesus really is the best thing not just *since* sliced bread, but *before* as well!

Abide in me and my words

JOHN 8:31; 15:4

Jesus is not just the bread that we eat; he is also the place where we live—our abiding place. He is the vine and we are the branches, and our task is to simply remain in the vine. If we abide there, we will be fruitful. "Abide in Me and I in you. As the branch cannot bear fruit of itself, unless it abides in the vine, so neither can you, unless you abide in Me" (15:4-5). These verses embody the idea of a double abiding: We abide in Christ, and he abides in us. Sap, like the Holy Spirit, courses through the branches, but when that sap runs dry we must anticipate being pruned—or even worse, cut off altogether! Don't worry if you are just experiencing a winter season, but watch out—dry sticks make excellent fire wood!

How do we abide? Well, both of our key passages here indicate that it is the words of Jesus which have a crucial part to play: "If you abide in *Me* and *My words* abide in you" (15:7, emphasis added), and "If you abide in *My word*" (8:31). Did you notice that double abiding once again? This time it is the words of Jesus which must abide in us. This can only happen if we abide in his words. Hopefully, this book has been helping you to see how key this process is. We need to let his words soak into every area of our lives—teaching us, shaping us, stretching us, inspiring us and making us fruitful. So, here we have it—this is the very heartbeat of our apprenticeship and proves our discipleship— "If you abide in My word, then you are truly disciples of Mine" (8:31) says Jesus. He goes on to say that you shall know the truth and the truth will set you free (v 32), really free (v 36).

I love the story that is told of David Livingstone, the missionary who worked in Africa. Apparently he commissioned a stamp to be made for sealing his letters; it read, "Christ in me the Living-Stone." [15] How neatly this captures the sense of double abiding: me in Christ and Christ in me. This is not an intermittent experience but a continual, constant, habitual

> This process proves our discipleship:
> "If you abide in my word, then you are truly disciples of Mine."

remaining in Christ, allowing the Holy Spirit to habitually, constantly, continually fill us with his life. What would happen if a farmer were to dig the potatoes out of the ground every other week to check their growth then replant them? We can't afford to take any time out of Christ, or his words, if we expect a fruitful season!

98

Walk in the light

JOHN 12:35

Walk while you have the light, that darkness may not overtake you; he who walks in the darkness does not know where he goes. While you have the light, believe in the light, in order that you may become sons of the light" (John 12:35–36). These two verses contain four simple injunctions concerning the light: we *have* the light, we *believe* in the light, we *walk* in the light, and we *become sons* of the light. So light characterizes everything about our lives. If we don't have light then darkness overcomes us, and if we walk in the dark we don't know where we are going. If we have the light, that light always overcomes the darkness: there is no contest between light and darkness—light always has the victory and darkness always flees. When we enter a darkened room it isn't necessary to gather up the darkness: it just melts away as we turn on the light (John 1:5).

> Four simple injunctions concerning the light:
> we have the light, we believe in the light,
> we walk in the light, and we become sons of the light.

Light gives us the ability to see, enabling us to find our way. Without the light we stumble and fall, having no way to register what is around or ahead of us. Light illuminates the way forward and enables us to clearly see the needs of those around us. The transition through *having*, to *believing*, to *walking*, to *being* the light not only impacts our own lives, but simultaneously provides a source of illumination for others. Jesus said that he was the light of the world, and anyone following him would not walk in darkness but would have the light of life (John 8:12). So too, we provide a certain brightness for the world. Not everyone would walk in our light, of course, for there are those that love darkness and would hate to come into the light, because it would expose their wickedness and evil deeds (John 3:19–20).

We should love the light. That means exposing our darkened hearts to the radiance of his light—and also requires that we live in the light with our fellow brothers and sisters. It has been said that "sin breeds in the darkness," so the more we live in the light the less likely it will be for sin to establish a foothold. Sometimes opening up our hearts to others is the only way to let in the light. John said in his epistle, "If we live in the light we have fellowship one with another" (1 John 1:7). "The one who says he is in the light and yet hates his brother is in darkness until now. The one who loves his brother abides in the light" (1 John 2:9–20).

When Moses entered God's presence, his face shone with such brilliance that he needed to wear a veil because the Children of Israel couldn't bear looking on his face. Not a bad idea if people can't stand your face! I refer to your radiance of course!

99

Wash one another's feet

JOHN 13:14, 15, 17

I was once preaching at a Danish church with a membership of around five hundred, when midway through the evening, the leader turned to address me. "Graham," he said, "I hope your feet are clean, because we are about to wash one another's feet." I seem to remember making some kind of quip that it would surely defeat the purpose if my feet were already clean! However, after a very moving time during which everyone washed someone's feet, I asked for the purpose of the exercise. The church leader looked aghast and remarked, "I thought Jesus told us to do it!" Being unable to summon up a speedy response I lamely replied, "Oh yes, so he did!"

Had I thought more quickly, I could have explained that this was a cultural command. It was customary to wash off the grime that glued itself to hot, sweaty feet which were protected only by lacy sandals. The environment would have been more than just dusty: the streets probably ran with animal—and human—excrement. For them it was essential, but for us it is less appropriate, with our modern streets, modern shoes, and a freezing cold climate! For them foot-washing symbolised servant-hood and humility, whereas for us it is just plain embarrassing. In fact, today I imagine it would demand as much humility to allow our feet to be washed by a brother as it would for us to wash his feet. Perhaps that is why Peter pulled back exclaiming, "Never shall you wash my feet!" But Jesus replied, "If I don't wash your feet you have no part with me." Peter then asked that Jesus also wash his hands and head, but Jesus refused on the grounds that it is enough just to wash the feet if you have already taken a bath. I'm sure foot-washing alludes to the issue of ongoing forgiveness: we need to allow the Lord to cleanse us from the grime of the day.

In Biblical times, houseguests were welcomed with a foot-washing ceremony. Is this a Christian rite to be practiced at some special foot-washing service—perhaps an interesting welcome at the church door? Or is this more of a cultural "there and then" type command, which would have been carried out by a lowly servant? Servanthood is actually the key issue, so we should probably find some modern equivalents. How about washing dishes, or washing one another's cars, or polishing one another's shoes? But having said all this,

> How about washing dishes, or washing one another's cars, or polishing one another's shoes?
> But having said all this, perhaps we should wash one another's feet.

perhaps we should still wash one another's feet, so that we can literally fulfil this command too! I am all for reviving this custom, and allowing it to once more express what it did in Jesus's day. Perhaps washing a brother's feet might actually help him shake the dust off his feet —a prophetic action to bring healing and forgiveness.

100

If you believe in God believe also in me

JOHN 14:1

Here is another two-part command: the first statement says, "Do not let your heart be troubled," and the second follows with, "If you believe in God believe also in me." The context of these imperatives is Jesus's prediction of Peter's denial—"The cock shall not crow until you have denied me three times." Peter so adamantly believed that he would have followed Jesus literally anywhere—even into death! The conversation had been so strange that it was beginning to unnerve the disciples. Jesus had announced he was going to a place to which they could not follow—but they would do so later. Although this seemed to be a little cryptic, the disciples certainly understood that Jesus was referring to death. Only Jesus can look death in the face and say, "do not be troubled."

Our hearts should not be troubled, because he has gone before us to prepare our place: in his Father's house there are many mansions, and he will receive us to himself. Where he has gone, there we will also go. These are bold, confident statements about life after death—hence the second part of this command—trust me: "If you believe in God believe also in me." The disciples, however, were still unsure and asked, "Lord, we do not know where you are going, and how can we know the way?" Jesus answers, "I am the way, and the truth, and the life, no man comes to the Father but through me." This Amazing Statement embodies so many truths that we don't have sufficient space to unpack. Suffice it to say that if you want to know God as Father, Jesus is the key! I have often heard people say that all religions lead to God. Well perhaps they do in some way or other, BUT only Jesus can lead us to God as our Father, and interestingly no other world religion would refer to God as "Father." "If you believe in God believe also in me." Why? Because Jesus says, "If you have known me, you have known the *Father*," and again "If you have seen me you have seen the *Father*" (emphasis added). "Do you not believe that I am in the *Father* and the *Father* is in me?" "Believe me, I am in the

> Only Jesus can look death in the face and say, 'Do not be troubled.' He has gone before us to prepare our place: in his Father's house there are many mansions.

Father and the *Father* is in me." To believe in God is the very same thing as to believe in Jesus! If you find this difficult to believe, then study the works of Jesus. Believe on account of the works themselves, because the Father dwelling in Jesus is the one who does those works. That is precisely why no one else ever did the amazing things Jesus did—so believe in him! To trust in Jesus is the way to put your trust in God. To follow Jesus and all his commands outlined here is the way to follow the Father's will for our lives.

> I believe you are the way, the truth and the life

A Real Apprentice

101

Love one another

JOHN 15:12, 17

We have already considered various aspects of love. We have looked at how we should love God with all the heart and mind, etc. We have thought about what it means to love our neighbors as we love ourselves, and we have also explored the crazy idea of loving our enemies. Now, almost at the end of Jesus's teaching material, he raises a final encouragement to love—this time to love one another. It is a suitable way to finish this selection of Jesus's commands, because love embraces all the other commandments. Hence Jesus introduces this verse by declaring, "This is *my* commandment" (emphasis added), as if there is really only one.

> The challenge is that we are to love one another as Christ loved us.

The "one another" in this commandment presumably refers to the other members of the body of Christ. He mentions this one last of all the *love* statements because it is the easiest to do…or is it? The challenge is that we are to love one another as Christ loved us. This standard seems infinitely higher than the sanction to love our neighbor, which is akin to loving in the way we love ourselves: this is reasonably attainable. But to love in the way that Jesus loved us is not quite so easy—particularly when we consider his own definition—"Greater love has no man than this; that he *lay down his life* for his friends" (emphasis added). Christ's love was self-sacrificing: it put others' interests before his own: it was a giving love, a caring love, a serving love, a praying love—a dying love.

It wasn't just a love that laid down life in *death*, but a love that laid down life in *life*. He didn't just *die* for others—he lived for others *before* he died for them. How about that for a challenge?

John 15:9–17 highlights the close interrelationship between obeying the commands of Jesus and living in his love. "If you keep my commandments you will abide in my love, just as I have kept my Father's commandments and abide in his love." There is also an inseparable link between our loving Jesus and obeying him: "If you love me you will keep my commandments" (John 14:15): and when we do so, there are wonderful promises for us: The Father and the Son promise to make their abode with us (14:23); the Son also promises to disclose himself to us (14:21); and he declares us as his friends if we do what he commands (15:14). Perhaps a fitting finish would be to conclude with the prayer of Saint Paul: "May the Lord cause you to increase and abound in love for one another, and for all men, just as we also do for you" (1 Thess. 3:12). Amen.

ALL 303 COMMANDS OF JESUS IN THE GOSPELS

1) Why do you call me Lord and not do what I say (Luke 6:46–49 Implied)
2) Man shall not live by bread alone but by every word (Matt. 4:4; Luke 4:4)
3) You shall not put God to the test (Matt. 4:7; Luke 4:12)
4) You shall worship the Lord your God and serve only him (Matt. 4:10; Luke 4:8)
5) Repent for the kingdom of heaven is at hand (Matt. 4:17; Mark 1:15)
6) Repent and believe the Gospel (Mark 1:15; Luke 13:3; 5)
7) Follow me and I will make you fishers of men (Matt. 4:19; Mark 1:19; Luke 5:10)
8) Rejoice and be exceedingly glad, leap for joy, when persecuted (Matt. 5:12; Luke 6:23)
9) Rejoice in that your names are written, not demons subject (Luke 10:20)
10) Let your light so shine before men that they may see your good works (Matt. 5:16; Mark 4:24, Luke 8:16; Luke 11:33; Luke 12:35)
11) Have salt in yourselves (Mark 9:50)
12) Your righteousness must exceed the Pharisees to enter Kingdom of Heaven (Matt. 5:20)
13) Do not be angry with your brother without cause (Matt. 5:22)
14) Before you leave your gift at the altar first be reconciled with your brother (Matt. 5:24)
15) Be at peace with one another (Mark 9:50)
16) Make friends with your opponent quickly (Matt. 5:25; Luke 12:58)
17) Do not lust in your heart (Matt. 5:28)
18) If your eye offends you pluck it out (Matt. 5:29; Mark 9:47; Matt. 18:9)
19) If your hand offends you cut it off (Matt. 5:30; Mark 9:43)

A Real Apprentice   219

20) You shouldn't divorce your wife (Matt. 5:32; Luke 19:9; Luke 16:18)
21) What God puts together let no man separate (Matt. 19:6 (Mark 10:9)
22) Make no oath at all (Matt. 5:34)
23) Let your yes be yes and your no be no (Matt. 5:37)
24) Resist not the one who is evil (Matt. 5:39)
25) Turn the other cheek Matt. 5:39; Luke 6:29)
26) If someone takes your shirt then give him your coat as well (Matt. 5:40; Luke 6:29)
27) Whoever takes away your goods don't ask for them back (Luke 6:35)
28) Go the second mile (Matt. 5:42)
29) Give to him who asks (Matt. 5:42)
30) Do not turn away those that want to borrow from you (Matt. 5:42)
31) Lend expecting nothing in return (Luke 6:35)
32) Love your enemies (Matt. 5:44; Luke 6:27, 35)
33) New commandment—That you love one another (John 13:34, 35; 15:12, 17)
34) Pray for those that persecute you (Matt. 5:44)
35) Bless those that curse you Luke 6:28)
36) Be perfect as your Father in heaven is perfect (Matt. 5:48)
37) Don't practise righteousness before people (Matt. 6:1)
38) Give in secret (Matt. 6:2–4)
39) Give in measure that you expect in return Luke 6:38)
40) Pray in secret (Matt. 6:4–6)
41) Don't pray with vain repetitions (Matt. 6:7)
42) Don't be like the hypocrites (Matt. 6:8)
43) Pray in this way— the Lord's prayer (Matt. 6:9–13)
44) They ought to pray and not lose heart Luke 18:1–8)
45) If you forgive your Father will forgive you (Matt. 6:14–15)
46) Fast in secret (Matt. 6:16–18 Luke 5:35)
47) Do not lay up treasure on earth (Matt. 6:19)
48) Beware against every form of greed Luke 12:15)

49) Sell your possessions and give to charity Luke 12:33)
50) Lay up treasure in heaven (Matt. 6:20; Luke 12:33)
51) You can't serve God and mammon (Matt. 6:24; Luke 6:13)
52) Watch out that your light be not darkness (Luke 11:35)
53) Do not be anxious for your life, what to eat or drink (Matt. 6:25; Luke 12:22, 29)
54) Look at the birds (Matt. 6:26; Luke 12:24)
55) Observe the lilies of the field (Matt. 6:28)
56) Seek first the kingdom of God (Matt. 6:33)
57) and his righteousness (Matt. 6:33)
58) Don't be afraid little flock Father's good pleasure to give you the kingdom (Luke 12:32)
59) Don't be anxious for tomorrow, for tomorrow will take care of itself (Matt. 6:34)
60) If worried and bothered about too many things, only one is necessary (Luke 10:41–42 Implied)
61) Do not judge or you will be judged (Matt. 7:1–2; John 7:24)
62) Condemn not and you will not be condemned (Luke 6:37)
63) Pardon and you will be pardoned (Luke 6:37)
64) Be merciful as your Father in heaven is merciful (Luke 6:36)
65) Take care how you hear, your standard will be measured to you (Mark 4:24)
66) Take the log out of your own eye then help your brother (Matt. 7:3–5; Luke 6:41)
67) Take the log out of your brother's eye (Matt. 7:5; Luke 6:42)
68) Do not give what is holy to the dogs (Matt. 7:6)
69) Ask and it will be given to you (Matt. 7:7; Luke 11:9; John 15:7; 16:24)
70) Seek and you will find (Matt. 7:7; Luke 11:9)
71) Knock and the door will be opened unto you (Matt. 7:7; Luke 11:9)
72) Have faith in God (Mark 11:22)
73) Ask believing you have received (Mark 11:24)
74) Ask the Father in my Name (John 15:16; 16:23)
75) Your faith has saved you, go in peace (Luke 7:50)

76) Treat others as you want to be treated (Matt. 7:12; Luke 6:31)
77) Enter by the narrow gate (Matt. 7:13; Luke 13:24)
78) Beware of false prophets (Matt. 7:15)
79) Do the will of the Father (Matt. 7:21 Implied; Mark 3:35; John 7:17)
80) Everyone who hears and does my words is like a wise man on a rock (Matt. 7:24–27; Luke 6:47)
81) Much is required from everyone who has been given much (Luke 12:47–48)
82) Listen—nothing going in to a man can defile him (Mark 7:14–23)
83) Go your way and let it be done as you have believed (Matt. 8:13, 9:29)
84) Let the dead bury the dead (Matt. 8:22; Luke 9:60)
85) No-one puts his hand on the plough and turns back (Luke 9:62)
86) Follow Me (Matt. 9:9; Mark 2:14; Luke 5:27; 9:54; John 10:27; 21:19, 23)
87) If any one serves me let him follow me (John 12:26)
88) I desire mercy and not sacrifice (Matt. 9:13; 12:7)
89) Put new wine into new wineskins (Matt. 9:17; Mark 2:21-22; Luke 5:36–38)
90) Beseech the Lord of Harvest to send out laborers (Matt. 9:38; Luke 10:2)
91) As you go preach saying the kingdom of heaven is at hand (Matt. 10:7; Luke 10:9)
92) Proclaim the kingdom of God (Luke 9:2)
93) Go home and tell your friends (Mark 5:19; Luke 8:39)
94) Go and report what you have seen and heard (Luke 7:22)
95) Heal the sick. (Matt. 10:8; Luke 9:2; Luke 10:9)
96) Raise the dead. (Matt. 10:8)
97) Cleanse lepers. (Matt. 10:8)
98) Cast out demons (Matt. 10:8; Mark 16:17)
99) Do not hinder those casting out demons in the name of Jesus (Luke 9:50)

100) I have given you authority to tread upon scorpions, and all power of the enemy (Luke 10:19)
101) Freely you have received, freely give (Matt. 10:8)
102) Do not acquire gold, silver or copper (Matt. 10:9; Luke 10:4)
103) Don't take a bag, two tunics, sandals, or staff (Matt. 10:10; Luke 9:3)
104) Don't take any bread (Mark 6:8; Luke 9:3)
105) In each city enquire who in it is worthy and abide there (Matt. 10:11)
106) Stay where you start, not going from house to house (Matt. 10:12; Mark 6:10; Luke 10:7)
107) As you enter a house give it your greeting of peace (Matt. 10:13; Luke 10:4)
108) Eat and drink whatever is put before you (Luke 10:7–8)
109) Greet no one along the way (Luke 10:4)
110) When rejected let your peace return to you (Matt. 10:13; Luke 10:6)
111) When rejected—leave that place (Matt. 10:14; Mark 6:11; Luke 9:5)
112) When they do not receive you nor your words shake off the dust (Matt. 10:14; Mark 6:11; Luke 9:5)
113) Wipe off the dust that clings from the city yet the kingdom has come near (Luke 10:11)
114) Be as wise as serpents and as harmless as doves (Matt. 10:16)
115) Go—I send you out as lambs (Matt. 10:16; Luke 10:3)
116) Beware of men for they deliver you up to the courts (Matt. 10:17; Mark 13:9; Luke 12:11; 21:12
117) Do not become anxious as to what to say as it will be given to you (Matt. 10:19–20; Mark 13:11; Luke 12:11; 21:14)
118) When they persecute you in this city flee to the next (Matt. 10:23)
119) Do not fear them, everything covered shall be revealed (Matt. 10:26)
120) What I tell you in darkness speak in the light (Matt. 10:27)

121) What I whisper in your ear proclaim from the roof tops (Matt. 10:27)
123) Do not fear those that can kill the body (Matt. 10:28; Luke 12:4)
124) Rather fear him who has power to cast soul and body into hell (Matt. 10:28; Luke 12:5)
125) Do not fear, you are worth more than many sparrows (Matt. 10:31; Luke 12:7)
126) Don't be ashamed of me or my words (Matt. 10:32-33; Mark 8:38; Luke 9:26; 12:9)
127) If you confess me before men I will confess you (Luke 12:8 Implied)
128) Do not think I came to bring peace but a sword (Matt. 10:34)
129) He who loves family more than me is not worthy of me (Matt. 10:37 Implied)
130) If anyone does not hate father, mother, wife, children....he cannot be a disciple (Luke 14:26 Implied)
131) He who does not take up his cross and follow me is not worthy (Matt. 10:38 Implied Luke 14:27)
132) He who finds his life shall lose it. He who has lost his life finds it (Matt. 10:39 Implied; Luke 9:24; 17:33)
133) Whoever receives me receives him who sent me (Matt. 10:40; Luke 9:48)
134) Whoever gives a cup of cold water receives a reward (Matt. 10:42 Implied; Mark 9:41)
135) Come aside and rest awhile (Mark 6:31)
136) He who has ears to hears let him hear: (Matt. 11:15)
137) Come to me all that labor and are heavy-laden (Matt. 11:28)
138) Take my yoke upon you and learn of me (Matt. 11:29)
139) Learn from me, I am meek and lowly (Matt. 11:29)
140) Either make the tree good and it's fruit good, or make it bad (Matt. 12:33)
141) Every careless word you shall render account for in judgment (Matt. 12:36 Implied)

142) By your words you shall be justified or condemned (Matt. 12:37 Implied)
143) Behold something greater than Jonah is here (Matt. 12:41)
144) Behold something greater than Solomon is here (Matt. 12:42)
145) Behold my mother, my brothers, who do the will of my Father. (Matt. 12:49–50)
146) Behold the sower went out to sow (Matt. 13:3-8; Mark 4:3)
147) Hear then the parable of the sower (Matt. 13:18)
148) Take heed, to whoever has shall more be given (Luke 8:18)
149) Let these words sink into your ears, the Son of man will be delivered (Luke 9:44)
150) Honor your father and mother (Matt. 15:4-7; Mark 7:10)
151) Honor the Lord with the heart not just lip service (Matt. 15:8; Mark 7:6 Implied)
152) Don't teach as commands the precepts of men (Matt. 15v9; Mark 7:7–8, 13)
153) Hear and understand it is what comes out of man that defiles him (Matt. 15:10)
154) Leave them alone, blind guides of the blind (Matt. 15:14)
155) Watch and beware of the leaven of the Pharisees (Matt. 16:6; Mark 8:15; Luke 12:1)
156) Whatever you bind on earth is bound in heaven (Matt. 16:19; 18:18)
157) First bind the strong man then plunder his goods (Mark 3:27)
158) Whatever you loose on earth is loosed in heaven (Matt. 16:19)
159) If anyone wishes to come after me, deny, take up your cross and follow me (Matt. 16:24)
160) He must take up his cross daily (Luke 9:23)
161) Whoever wishes to save his life shall lose it, but whoever loses (Matt. 16:25)
162) Don't blaspheme the Holy Spirit (Mark 2:29; Luke 12:10 Implied)
163) All things are possible to him who believes (Mark 9:23)
164) Unless you be converted and become like children not enter kingdom (Matt. 18:3; Mark 10:15)

165) Whoever humbles himself as a child is the greatest in the kingdom (Matt. 18:4 Implied)
166) Whoever receives a child in my name receives me (Matt. 18:5; Mark 9:37; Luke 9:48; 18:17
167) Whoever stumbles a child should be drowned in the sea (Implied not Applied!) (Matt. 18:6; Mark 9:42)
168) If your hand or foot causes you to stumble cut it off (Matt. 18:8; Mark 9:45; Luke 17:2)
169) See that you do not despise these little ones (Matt. 18:10)
170) If your brother sins reprove him (Matt. 18:15; Luke 17:3)
171) If he repents forgive him (Luke 17:3)
172) If he does not listen take someone with you (Matt. 18:16)
173) If he refuses to listen tell it to the church (Matt. 18:17)
174) If he refuses to listen to the church let him be as a gentile to you (Matt. 18:17)
175) Forgive your brother until seventy times seven (Matt. 18:21; Luke 17:4)
176) What God puts together let no man separate (Matt. 19:6)
177) Whoever divorces, except for immorality, and marries another commits adultery (Matt. 19:9)
178) Accept being a eunuch if you are able (Matt. 19:12)
179) Let the children come, do not hinder them, for the kingdom belongs to such (Matt. 19:14; Mark 10:14)
180) If you wish to enter into life keep the commandments (Matt. 19:17; Luke 18:20)
You shall not: murder, commit adultery, steal, or lie, (Matt. 19:18; Mark 10:19)
Honor your father and mother, and love your neighbor as yourself (Matt. 19:19)
181) Do not lord it over others, whoever wishes to be great must serve (Matt. 20:26; Mark 10:43; Luke 12:26)
182) The greatest must be as the youngest (Luke 22:26)
183) Whoever wishes to be first must be as the slave (Matt. 20:27; Mark 9:35; Mark 10:44)
184) If you have faith, say to this mountain be cast into the sea and

it will (Matt. 21:21) If you have faith as a mustard seed, say to this mountain be removed (Matt. 17:20)

185) All things you ask in prayer believing, you shall have them (Matt. 21:22)
186) Go into the highways and byways (Matt. 22:9)
187) Render unto Caesar the things that are Caesar's (Matt. 22:21; Mark 12:17; Luke 20:25)
188) Render unto God the things which are God's (Matt. 22v21; Mark 12:17; Luke 20:25)
189) You shall love the Lord your God with all your heart. (Matt. 22:37; Mark 12:30; Luke 10:27)
190) You shall love the Lord your God with all your soul. (Matt. 22v37; Mark 12:30; Luke 10:27)
191) You shall love the Lord your God with all your mind (Matt. 22v37; (Mark 12v30; Luke 10:27
192) You shall love the Lord your God with all your strength (Mark 12:30; Luke 10:27)
193) You shall love your neighbor as yourself (Matt. 22:39; Mark 12:31)
194) Do this and live (Luke 10:28)
195) Go and do likewise (Be a good Samaritan) (Luke 10:37)
196) My house should be a house of prayer for all nations (Matt. 21v13; Mark 11:17; Luke 19:46)
197) Do what they say and observe it (Matt. 23:3;John 2:16)
198) Do not do what they do (Matt. 23:3)
199) Beware of the scribes who love respect/greetings/chiefseats/ longprayers/devour widow's houses/ broaden their phylacteries (Mark 12:38; Matt. 23:5)
200) Do not be called teacher (Matt. 23:8-10)
201) Do not be called leader (Matt. 23:8-10)
202) Do not be called father (Matt. 23:8-10)
203) The greatest shall be as a servant (Matt. 23:11)
204) Humble yourself (Matt. 23:23; Luke 14:11; 18:14)
205) Tithe your mint, dill and cummin (Matt. 23:23)

206) Don't neglect the weightier provisions of the law, including justice (Matt. 23:23)
207) Don't neglect the weightier provisions of the law, including mercy (Matt. 23:23)
208) Don't neglect the weightier provisions of the law, including faithfulness (Matt. 23:23)
209) Take heed that no man deceive you (Matt. 24:4; Mark 13:5; Mark 13:23)
210) Do not be troubled by wars and rumours (Matt. 24:6; Mark 13:7; Luke 21:9)
211) Don't let your love grow cold (Matt. 24:12 Implied)
212) Endure to the end and you will be saved (Matt. 24:13 Implied)
213) When the gospel is preached to the whole world then the end shall come (Matt. 24:14; Mark 13:10)
214) Let the reader understand (Matt. 24:15 Poss. Matthew's command)
215) On housetop don't go down into house (Mark 13:15)
216) In the field don't return for your clothes (Mark 13:16)
217) Pray that your flight not be in winter or on the Sabbath (Matt. 24:20)
218) If someone says here is Christ don't believe them (Matt. 24:23; Mark 13:6; Mark 13:21; Luke 21:8)
219) If they say Christ is there—Go not forth (Matt. 24:26; Luke 17:23)
220) Learn the parable of the fig tree (Matt. 24:32)
221) Recognize that He is near even at the door (Matt. 24:32)
222) Watch for you know not at what hour (Matt. 24:42; Mark 13:33-37)
223) Be you also ready (Matt. 24:44; Luke 12:35, 40)
224) Be a faithful servant (Matt. 24:46 Implied)
225) Be alert with oil in your lamps (Matt. 25:1–13 Implied)
226) Use your talents (Matt. 25:11–30; Luke 12:48 Implied)
227) Feed the hungry (Matt. 25:35-37)
228) Give what is on the plate to the poor (Luke 11:41)

229) Visit those that are sick (Matt. 25:35-37)
230) Clothe the naked (Matt. 25:35-37)
231) Visit those in prison (Matt. 25:35-37)
232) Give the thirsty something to drink (Matt. 25:35–37)
233) Invite the stranger in (Matt. 25:35-37)
234) Do good to the poor whenever you wish (Matt. 26:11; Mark 14:7; John 12:8)
235) Take eat this is my body (Matt. 26:26; Mark 14:22; Luke 22:19; John 6:53)
236) Drink this cup (Matt. 26:27; Mark 14:24; Luke 22:17; John 6:53)
237) Watch and pray that you enter not into temptation (Matt. 26:41; Mark 14:38; Luke 22:40, 46)
238) Watch and pray to get strength to escape all these things (Luke 22:36)
239) Watch and pray to get strength to stand before the Son of Man (Luke 22:36)
240) Go into the world (Matt. 28:19)
241) As the Father has sent me so send I you (Implied John 20:21)
242) Make disciples of all nations (Matt. 28:19)
243) Baptize them in the name of Father Son and Holy Spirit (Matt. 28:19)
244) Teaching them to observe all that I have commanded (Matt. 28:20)
245) Preach the gospel to all creation (Mark 16:15)
246) Believe and be baptised are saved (Mark 16:16)
247) Speak in tongues (Mark 16:17)
248) Pick up serpents will not be hurt (Mark 16:18)
249) You can drink deadly poison and not be harmed (Mark 16:18)
250) Lay hands on the sick they will recover (Mark 16:18)
251) Don't take the best seats (Luke 14:8)
252) Take the lowest seat (Luke 14:10)
253) Invite the poor, crippled, lame, blind when you give a meal (Luke 14:13, 21)

254) Don't invite your brothers, relatives or rich neighbors for a meal (Luke 14:12)
255) Compel the homeless to come in (Luke 14:23)
256) First sit down and count the cost (Luke 14:28-32, Implied)
257) Give up all your own possessions (Luke 14:33)
258) Rejoice with me over the lost being found (Luke 15:6, 9)
259) Make friends by using money (Luke 16:9)
260) Say we are unworthy servants (Luke 17:10)
261) Permit the little children to come to me (Luke 18:16)
262) Behold the fig tree and all trees (Luke 21:29)
263) Recognize that the kingdom of God is come near (Luke 21:31)
264) Be on your guard that your hearts are not weighted down by dissipation (Luke 21:34)
265) Be on your guard that your hearts are not weighted down by drunkenness (Luke 21:34)
266) Be on your guard that your hearts are not weighted down by worries of life (Luke 21:34)
267) Take your purse (Luke 22:36)
268) Take your bag (Luke 22:36)
269) Buy yourself a sword (Luke 22:36)
270) Stay until you are endued with power from on high (Luke 24:49)
271) You shall bear witness also (John 15:27)
272) Unless you are born again cannot see the kingdom (John 3:3, 5)
273) Must worship in Spirit and Truth (John 4:24)
274) Don't say three months then harvest (John 4:35)
275) Lifts up your eyes look on the fields (John 4:35)
276) Do not marvel, all in the tombs shall hear his voice (John 5:28)
277) Do not work for food that perishes (John 6:27)
278) Work for food, which endures, to eternal life (John 6:27)
279) This is the work….believe on him whom he sent (John 6:29)
280) Do not grumble among yourselves (John 6:43)

281) If any one thirsty let him come to me and drink (John 7:37)
282) Go and sin no more (John 8:11)
283) Abide in my words then truly my disciples (John 8:31)
284) If Abraham's children then do the works of Abraham (John 8:39)
285) We must work the works (John 9:4)
286) Believe the works (John 10:38; 14:11)
287) Walk in the light (John 12:35)
288) Believe in the light (John 12:36)
289) Wash one another's feet (John 13:14, 15, 17)
290) Let not your heart be troubled (John 14:1)
291) If you believe in God believe in me (John 14:1)
292) Greater works shall you do (Implied) (John 14:12)
293) If you love me keep my commandments (John 14:15, 21 23; 15:10
294) Abide in me (John 15:4)
295) Go and bring forth fruit (John 15:16)
296) Remember the slave is not greater than his master (John 15:20)
297) Take courage I have overcome the world (John 16:33)
298) Receive the Holy Spirit (John 20:22)
299) Forgive sins they are forgiven (Implied) (John 20:23)
300) Whatever sins you retain shall be retained (Implied) (John 20:23)
301) Don't doubt but believe (John 20:27)
302) Feed my lambs (John 21:15, 17)
303) Be a shepherd to my lambs (John 21:16)

ENDNOTES

1) "This Little Light of Mine" is a gospel children's song by Harry Dixon Loes (1895–1965) in about 1920.
2) "Make way, make way" by Graham Kendrick released: 1986 (Make Way Music/Kingsway Music Ltd). www.grahamkendrick.co.uk/discography/carnival.php.
3) John W. (Jack) Carter, "Overcome Evil with Love." *Biblical Theology,* (2011), http://www.biblicaltheology.com.
4) Jim Elliot, *Journals of Jim Elliot,* ed. by Elisabeth Elliot (Revell 1978) 108.
5) WWJD — The phrase "What would Jesus do?" (often abbreviated to WWJD) became popular in the United States in the 1990s and as a personal motto for adherents of Evangelical Christianity. http://en.wikipedia.org.
6) 'Nothing in my hand I bring' hymn lyric in "Rock of Ages" (Augustus M. Toplady, 1740–1778).
7) The Alpha Course is a low-pressure, fun and informative course. An introduction to basic Christianity and to explore the meaning of life. uk-england.alpha.org
8) *Planet Earth* is a television series produced by the BBC Natural History Unit, first broadcast in the U. K. on BBC One in March 2006, narrated by David Attenborough and produced by Alastair Fothergill.
9) Hymn lyric, "Something lives in every hue," written in 1876 by George Robinson, entitled "I am His and He is mine."
10) Year of Jubilee — Leviticus 25.
11) Roger Forster — the pioneer and leader of Ichthus Christian Fellowship—a church-planting movement based in London. He was the former Chairman of the Evangelical Alliance UK.
12) Malcolm Gladwell, *Blink: The Power of Thinking Without Thinking* (Back Bay Books, Little, Brown, 2005), 320.
13) Poem by Alexander Pope (An Essay on Criticism English poet and satirist 1688–1744).

14) The number of kilometres of typewritten noughts was calculated by the Russian neuroanatomist, Professor Anokhin, quoted in *Awakening the Sleeping Giant*: By (authors) Marilyn Katzenmeyer and Gayle Moller (Corwin Press, September 2009).
15) Eugene Myers Harrison, *Giants of the Missionary Trail* (Scripture Press, Book Division, 1954). Quoting David Livingstone, "Christ in me the Livingstone."